Yolngu Mali
ABORIGINAL SPIRIT

Yolngu Mali
ABORIGINAL SPIRIT

Photographs by **Peter McConchie**

Text by **Milkayngu Mununggurr** and **Binmila Yunupingu**

Foreword by **Gatjil Djerrkura**

Assisted by the **Yothu Yindi Foundation**

VIKING

Viking
Penguin Books Australia Ltd
487 Maroondah Highway, PO Box 257
Ringwood, Victoria 3134, Australia
Penguin Books Ltd
Harmondsworth, Middlesex, England
Penguin Putnam Inc.
375 Hudson Street, New York, New York 10014, USA
Penguin Books Canada Limited
10 Alcorn Avenue, Toronto, Ontario, Canada M4V 3B2
Penguin Books (NZ) Ltd
Cnr Rosedale and Airborne Roads, Albany, Auckland, New Zealand
Penguin Books (South Africa) (Pty) Ltd
5 Watkins Street, Denver Ext. 4, 2094, South Africa
Penguin Books India (P) Ltd
11, Community Centre, Panchsheel Park, New Delhi 110 017, India

First published by Penguin Books Australia Ltd 2001

10 9 8 7 6 5 4 3 2 1

Copyright © photographs, the Yothu Yindi Foundation 2001;
main text, Milkayngu Mununggurr and Binmila Yunupingu;
introduction, Peter McConchie 2001; foreword, Gatjil Djerrkura 2001

The moral right of the authors has been asserted

All rights reserved. Without limiting the rights under copyright reserved above, no part of this publication may be reproduced, stored in or introduced into a retrieval system, or transmitted, in any form or by any means (electronic, mechanical, photocopying, recording or otherwise), without the prior written permission of both the copyright owner and the above publisher of this book.

Designed by Nikki Townsend, Penguin Design Studio
Typeset in Frutiger by Nikki Townsend, Penguin Design Studio
Printed and bound by Bookbuilders Limited, Hong Kong, China

National Library of Australia
Cataloguing-in-Publication data:

McConchie, Peter
Yolngu mali: Aboriginal spirit

  ISBN 0 670 88851 6.

  1. Yolgnu (Australian people) – Social life and customs.
  2. Aborigines, Australian – Northern Territory – Social life and customs.
  I. Mununggur, Milkayngu. II. Yunupingu, Binmila.
  III. Yothu Yindi Foundation. IV. Title.

  306.0899915

www.penguin.com.au

ACKNOWLEDGEMENTS

This book has been made possible with the help of the people of north-east Arnhem Land. Sincere thanks go to my Gumatj family and friends for their much valued assistance and care, in particular Nuliny Ganambarr, Lisa Yunupingu, Noonkai Yunupingu and Andrea Collins. Thanks also to Sandra Bardas, Ian Richardson and John Bennetts, whose support is greatly felt and deeply appreciated.

Peter McConchie

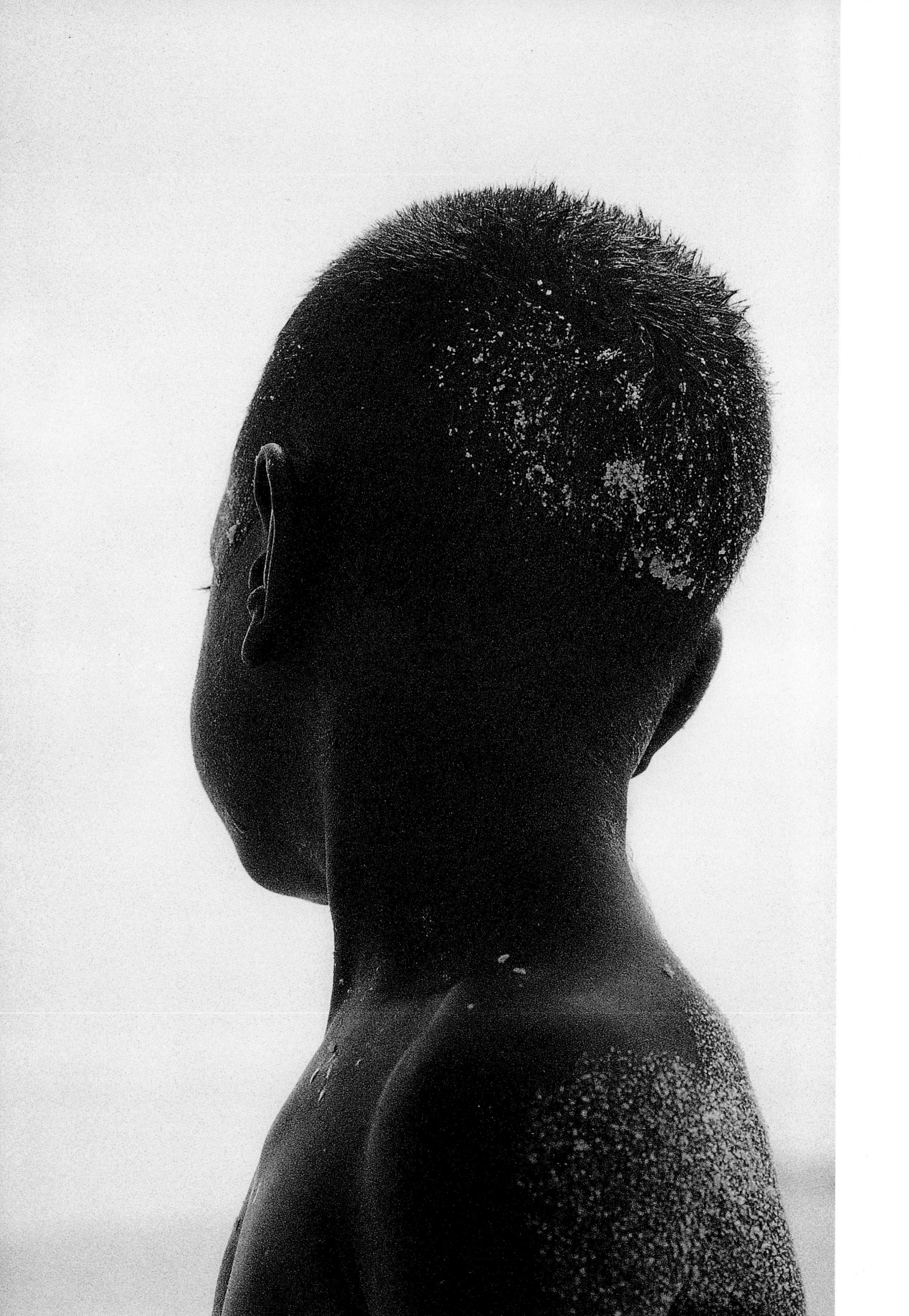

CONTENTS

Foreword	1
Introduction	2
Our Children	5
Growing Up	17
Family Stories	27
Ceremony	37
Timeless Women	43
Flowers, Stingrays and Turtles	55
Flying Fox	67
Wild Honey	73
Kangaroo Hunter	83
After Bushfire	89
Warrior	95
Glossary	112
List of Photographs	113

PUBLISHER'S NOTE

The text accompanying these photographs was transcribed from stories told by Milkayngu Mununggurr and Binmila Yunupingu, of the Yolngu people. Their spoken words have been edited only for clarity and length, with the intention being not to standardise their language but rather to preserve their Aboriginal voices.

The dotted keyline in the map below shows the approximate location of Yolngu territory.

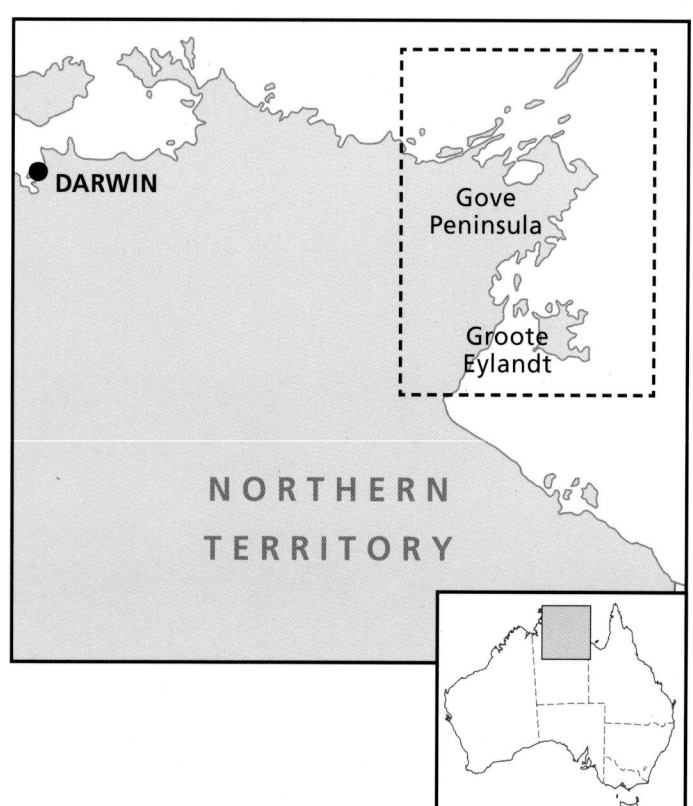

FOREWORD

When I think of photography, I think of the early pictures of my people in chains – in work gangs, in makeshift shacks made of anything people could find to make houses. I also think of the children in church homes, lined up like little soldiers, dressed like servants, removed from their families and stripped of culture and identity.

The camera was used to convince the world that the land was empty and unclaimed. Pictures of our country showed it to be a place devoid of people and artefacts of civilisation. There were no temples or pyramids or other forms of history which could be understood by white people as culture. What none cared to consider was that through our eyes the mountains, the deserts, the rivers and the seas were not vacant land. No one considered that they are our temples, our culture – they are us.

In later years the camera was used to reinforce the cruellest of stereotypes – the alcohol, the violence. Desperation dominated images of Aboriginal culture. No one wanted to show images of the strong families, the struggle to survive, the living beauty of our way and culture.

As you can imagine, we have learned to be careful of white people and cameras. It is for this reason that this book is unusual. This time the camera has not been pointed at us from across the cultural divide, but has instead travelled to our culture and worked within our framework of knowledge and understanding. This is why these pictures contain some of the simple joy, freedom and spirit I know as an Aboriginal man.

My hope is that viewing this work helps you to begin to unravel in your own mind some of the myths and the lies which were created to calm the conscience of the conquerors.

Gatjil Djerrkura OAM

INTRODUCTION

I had been contemplating photographing a story on traditional Aboriginal life for some time when in 1998 I had the pleasure of meeting Gatjil Djerrkura, Chair of the Aboriginal and Torres Strait Islander Commission, who granted me permission to proceed. Gatjil directed me to the Yolngu people of north-east Arnhem Land, a place very strong in traditional culture. There are many clan groups within the Yolngu, each with its own land, stories, songs, totems and dialect. Gatjil introduced me to Galarrwuy Yunupingu, a leader of the Gumatj clan, who is also head of the Northern Land Council and co-chair of the Yothu Yindi Foundation. He agreed to oversee my work.

I arrived in Arnhem Land in May 1998 and met Galarrwuy's brother, Noonkai Yunupingu, a Gumatj elder. Noonkai took me to his homeland Dhaniya, on the Gove Peninsula, and welcomed me into his family. I was given a Yolngu name, and for the next six months I lived either in the Yunupingu home or in my tent near the beach. May to November is the dry season in Arnhem Land, a time of near-perfect weather.

The Dhaniya area is a pristine land of stringybark forests and cycads that follow the shoreline of the peninsula. The cycad, which dates back to the days of Gondwanaland (the period when Australia was part of a larger supercontinent), has an important place in Yolngu culture; its seeds are used in the making of damper after first being leached to remove the poisons. On the other side of the forests is desert. These are the traditional hunting grounds of the Yolngu people, both land and sea. It was at Dhaniya and across the sea at Bawaka that most of this book was photographed. My equipment consisted of three 35mm black and white processors, a lightbox, 160 rolls of slide film, two cameras, assorted lenses, and a waterproof case. I took the processing equipment with me so that the images could be developed on location for approval.

Before I began work on the book, I used three rolls of film around the camp as a test, and invited the family to see the transparencies on the lightbox once the film was developed. I processed the first roll as I had a thousand others – it was unusable, the emulsion had ruined the images. I tried the second roll in a different processor and got the same result. When the third roll also proved useless, the people were disappointed and I was devastated; I thought I would have to leave Arnhem Land to sort the problem out. As I was rechecking my equipment, Noonkai calmly explained that, while I had received permission to photograph Yolngu culture from the Aboriginal leaders and from the Gumatj people themselves, I had not yet asked permission from the spirit of the land. I was told the spirit keeper's name, and that night I asked permission before falling asleep. The next day I tested another three rolls of film in the same three processors – and all the film was fine.

When photographing for this book I simply let the stories unravel in front of me. Every day someone would go fishing – for giant trevally, mackerel, barracuda or stingray. When the hunting went well there would be dugong or turtle, and, inland, kangaroo, goanna and flying fox. On my first trip hunting flying fox, twelve of us headed off in a boat to Mosquito Creek, an hour or so from Dhaniya. We cruised in slowly at midday when the flying foxes were asleep. Some of the young men were dropped off in the mangroves, armed with clubs and small, multi-pronged spears (they would eventually return with dozens of flying foxes between them). From the boat, an elder fired a couple of rounds from his shotgun into the tops of the mangroves and the flying foxes took to the sky in panic. Another man shot the foxes as they flew, and we then motored around and plucked them from the water, clubbing and spearing any that were still alive. As with everything I photographed, Noonkai Yunupingu advised me closely on what I should include and what I should not.

The Aboriginal world is about unity – between the natural and the spiritual, between the past and the present, between the people and their environment. *Aboriginal Spirit: Yolngu Mali* seeks to build a bridge between Indigenous and non-Indigenous cultures by celebrating the Yolngu way of life. A percentage of the sales of this book will go to the Yothu Yindi Foundation to assist in the development of the Garma Culture Centre, which teaches the Yolngu culture and knowledge.

Peter McConchie

OUR CHILDREN

When we go hunting the kids always want to come. We take them fishing. Best time to go fishing for mullet is when there's no moon. Take a torch and shine it and the fish come. Kids see what we do and they copy us and that's what they learn from.

Kids are gorgeous, they're really active, they play games. Everything in the city involves money, but up here things don't. Parents don't supervise their kids as much because they don't need to. Even swimming, the kids see a crocodile when it raises its head, but a balanda kid would think it was a log or something.

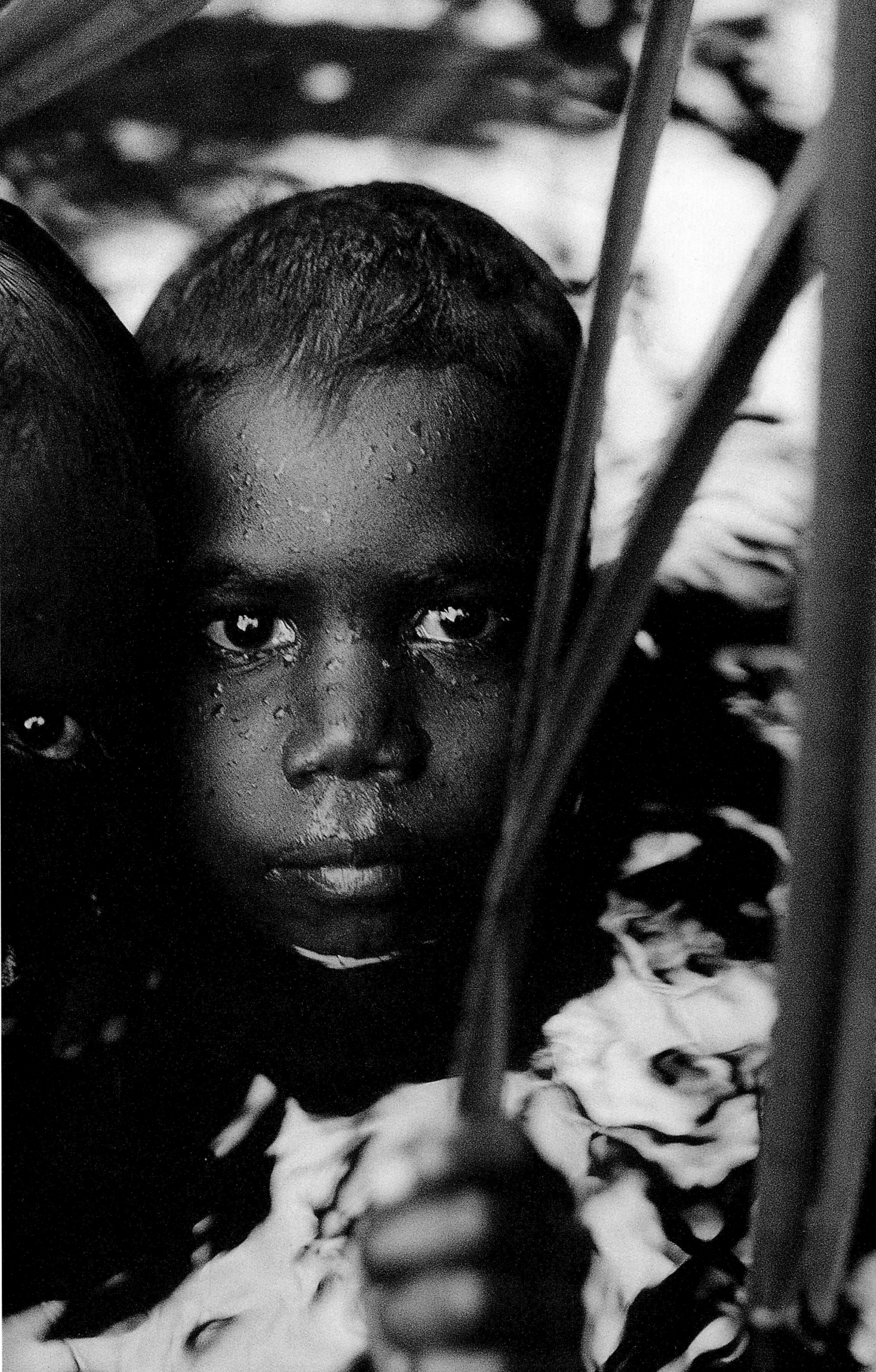

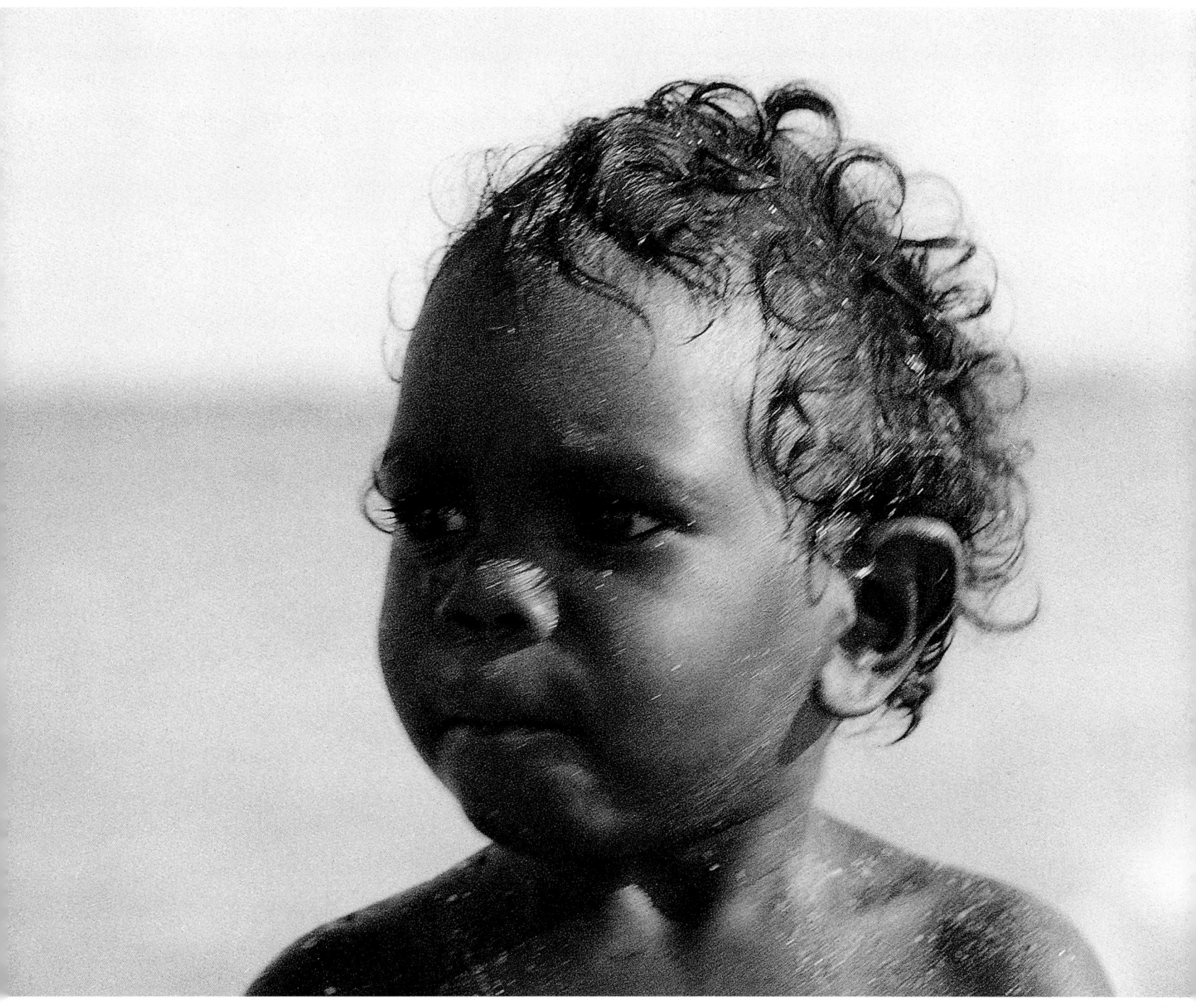

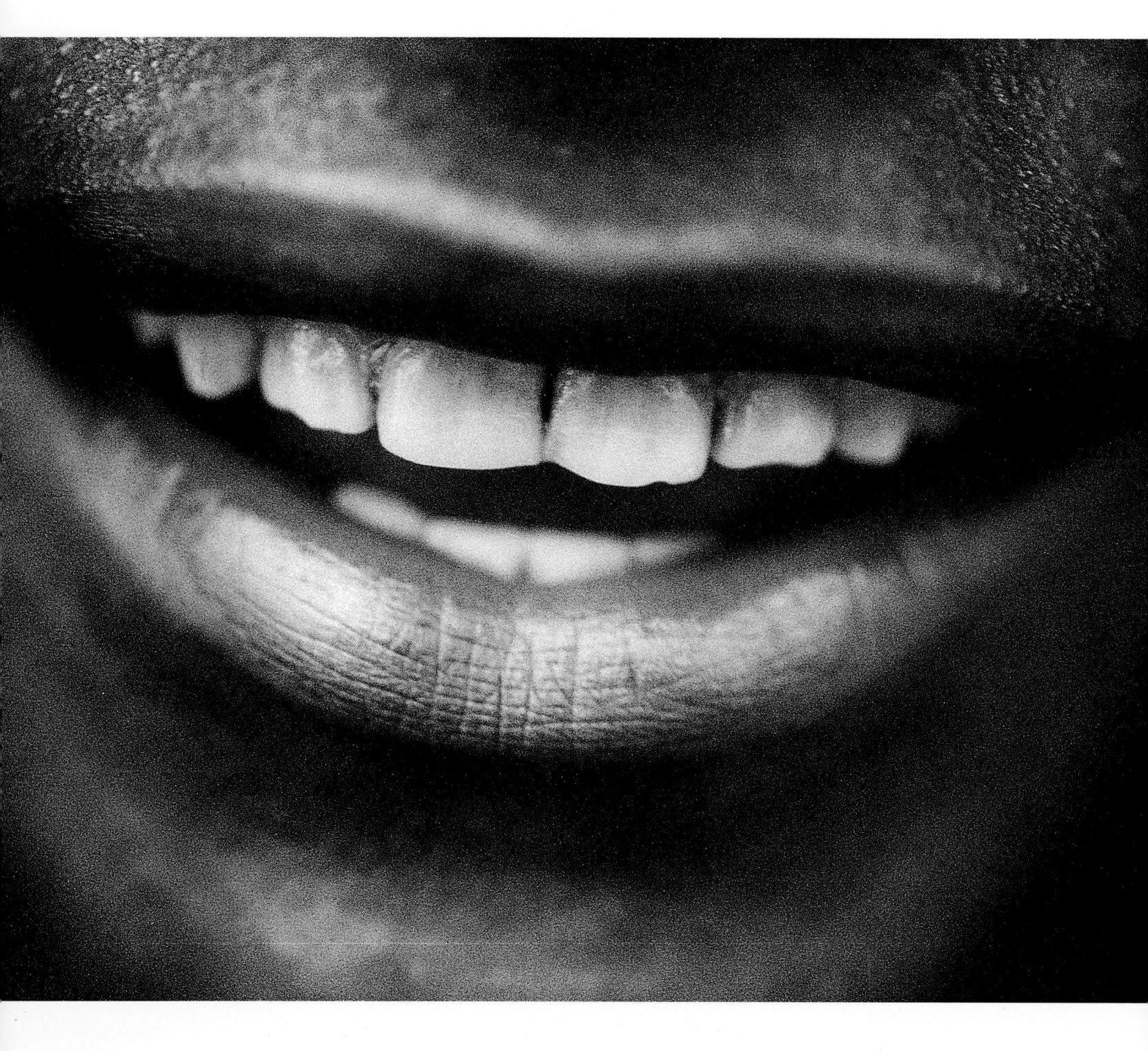

GROWING UP

When kids are little they don't get called their name, just their skin name. Then when they're older we use their name. Every person in a family is either Yirritja or Dhuwa, either one or the other. Every animal, every plant, everything in the sea and in the land, even the wind, sky, cloud, sun. Sun is Dhuwa, moon is Yirritja. The red reflection of sunset is Yirritja. Sunrise is Dhuwa. Us, stars, the Milky Way, it's all got stories, it's all either Dhuwa or Yirritja.

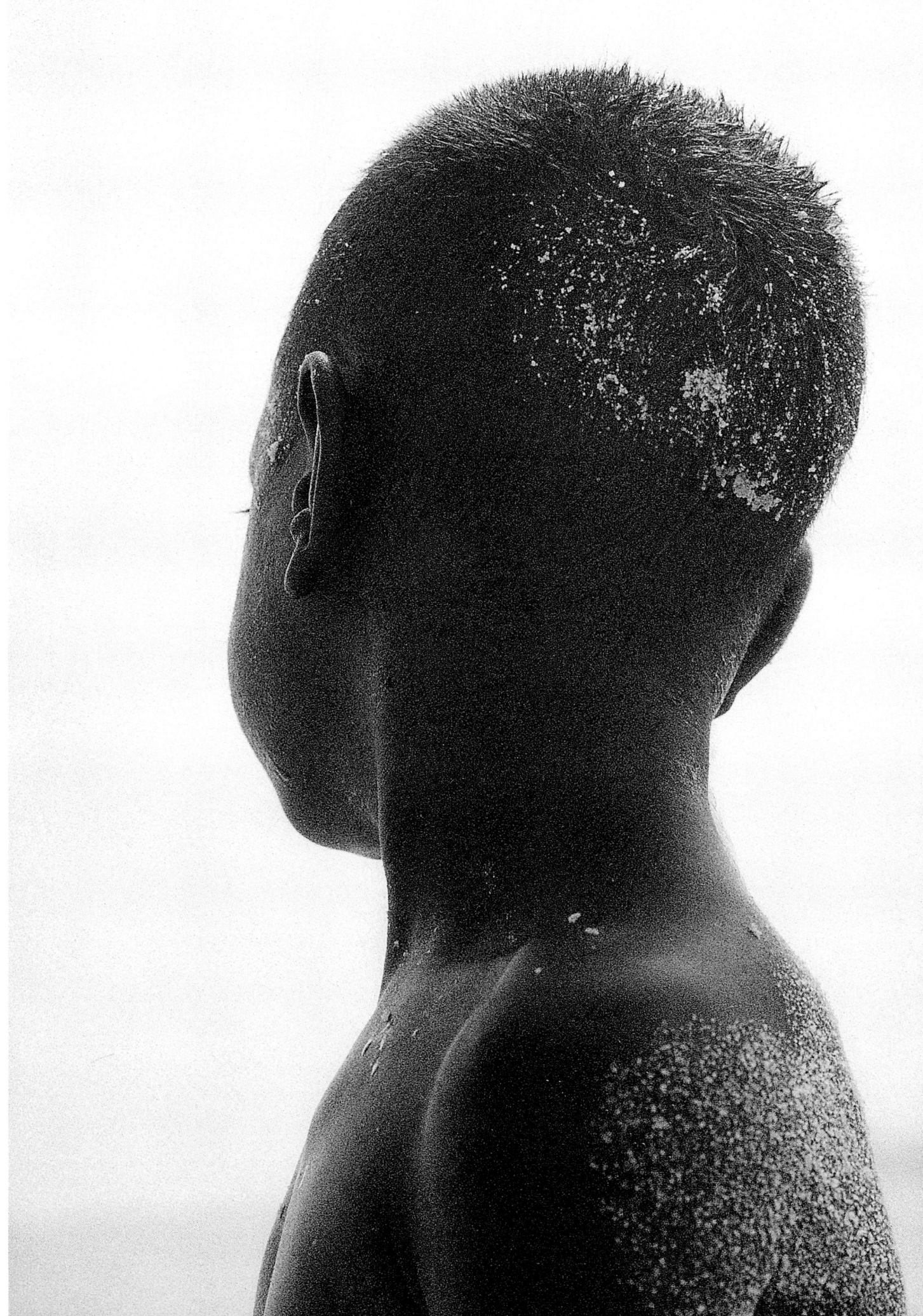

FAMILY STORIES

When there are big arguments the old ladies are the peacemakers, but they don't take sides. They stand in the middle, especially when two men argue. Men can have as many wives as they want, but depends on the wives too. If the first or second wife doesn't agree, it makes it hard on the husband. Women can't have more than one husband.

Women aren't going to go and hunt a roo, they don't use spears for hunting. Women would not get involved in a battle between two mobs, they would take care of the kids and take them to safety. A sibling cannot say another sibling's name, they call them brother or sister for respect.

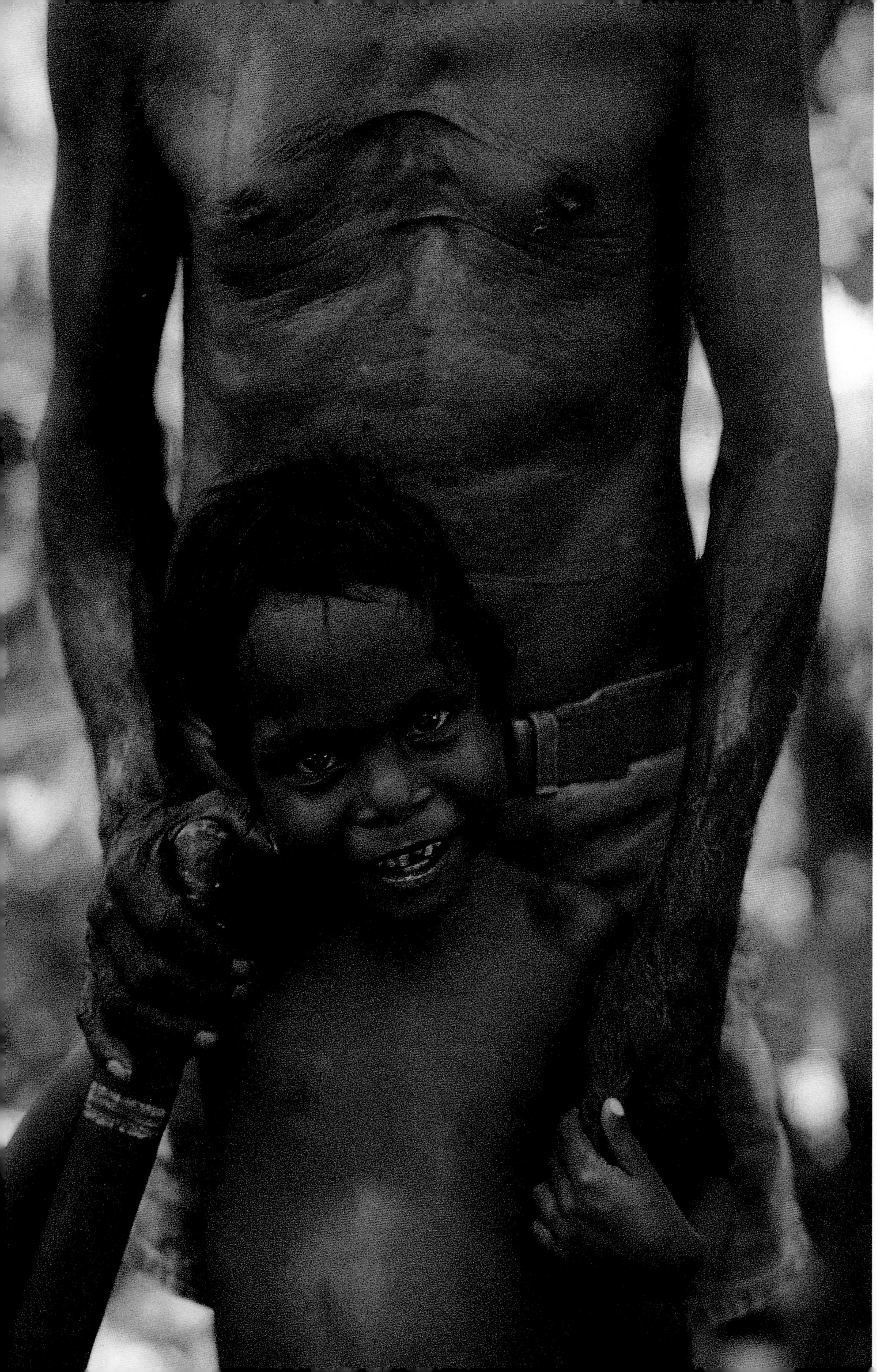

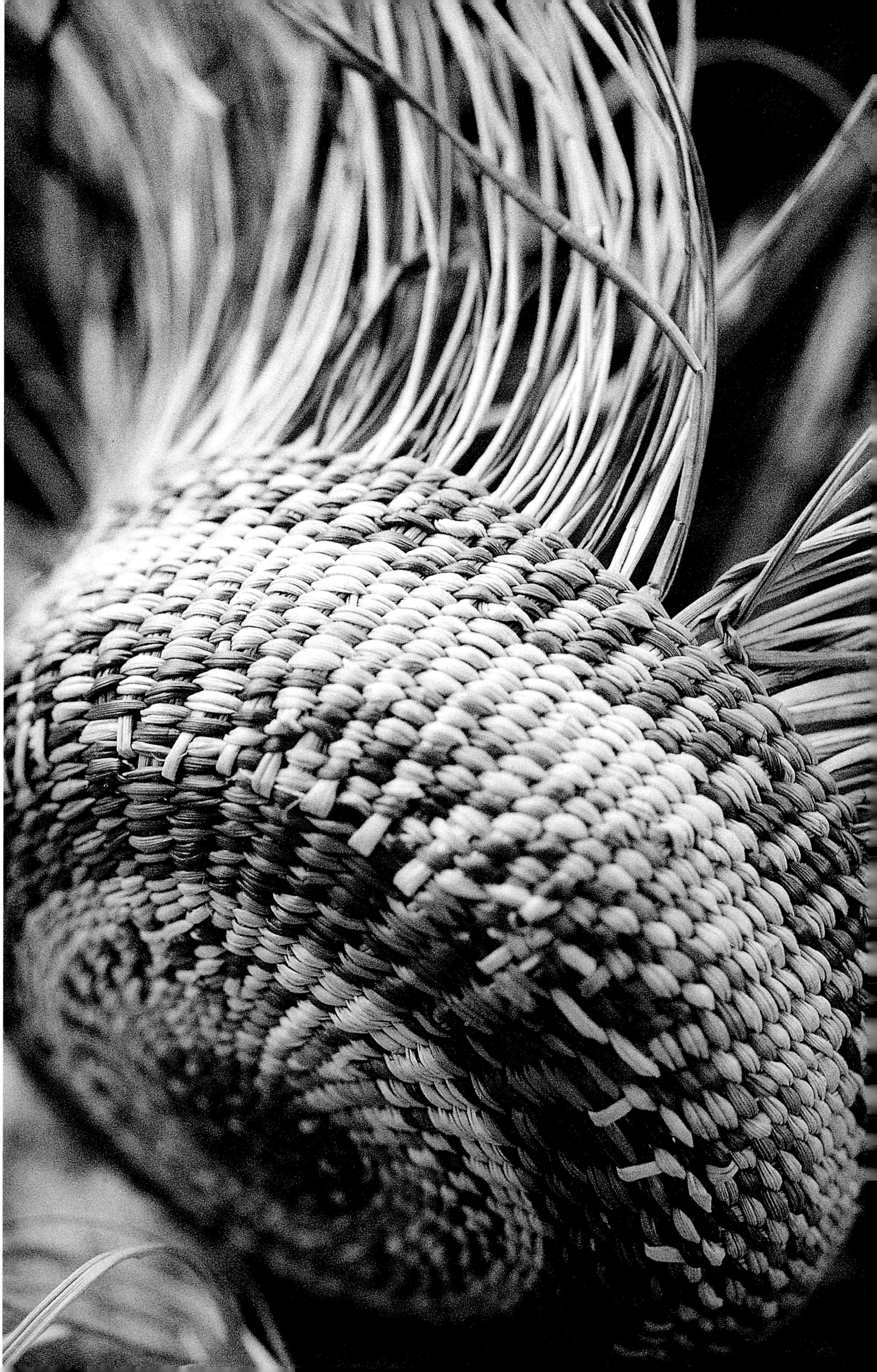

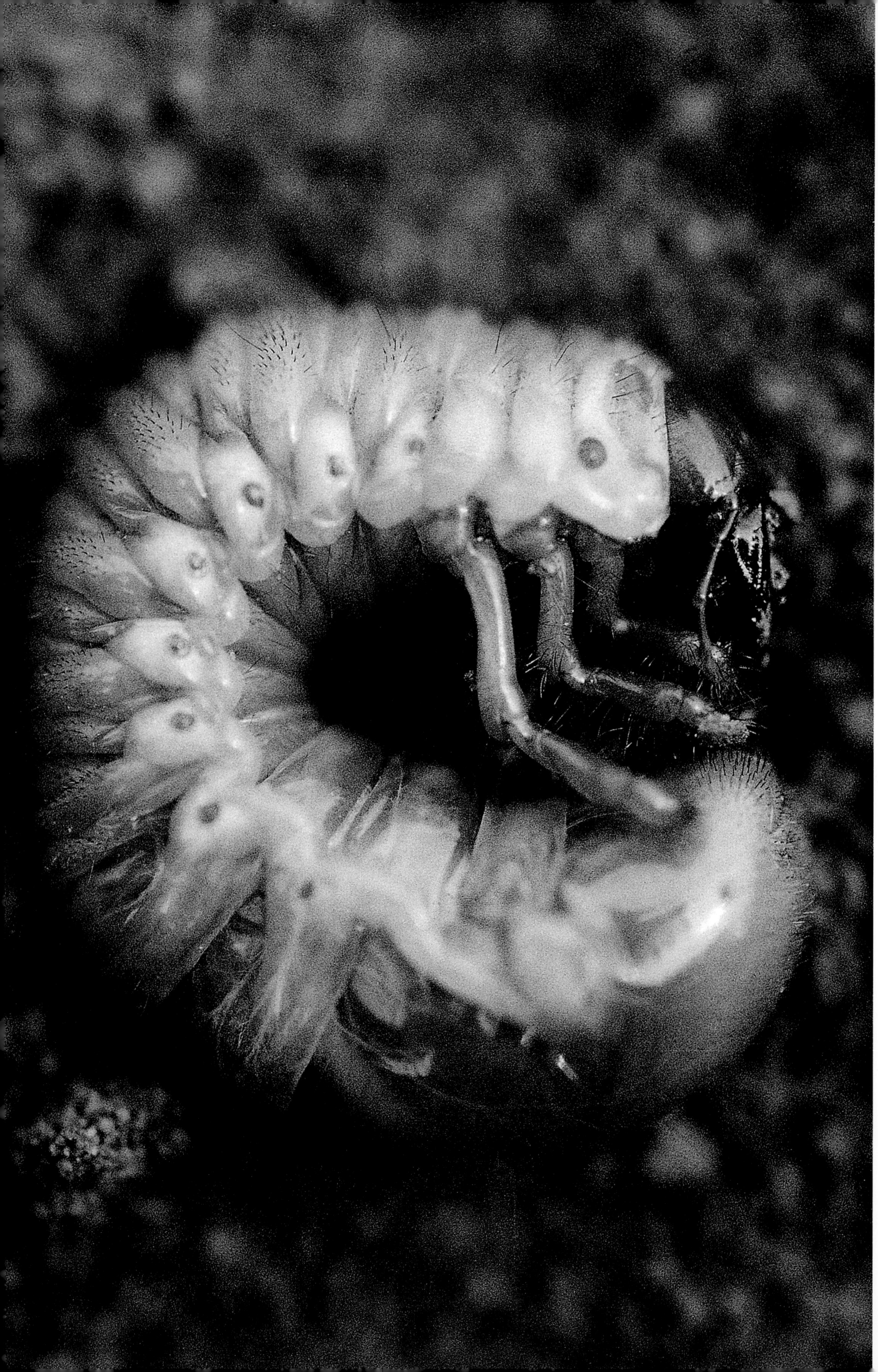

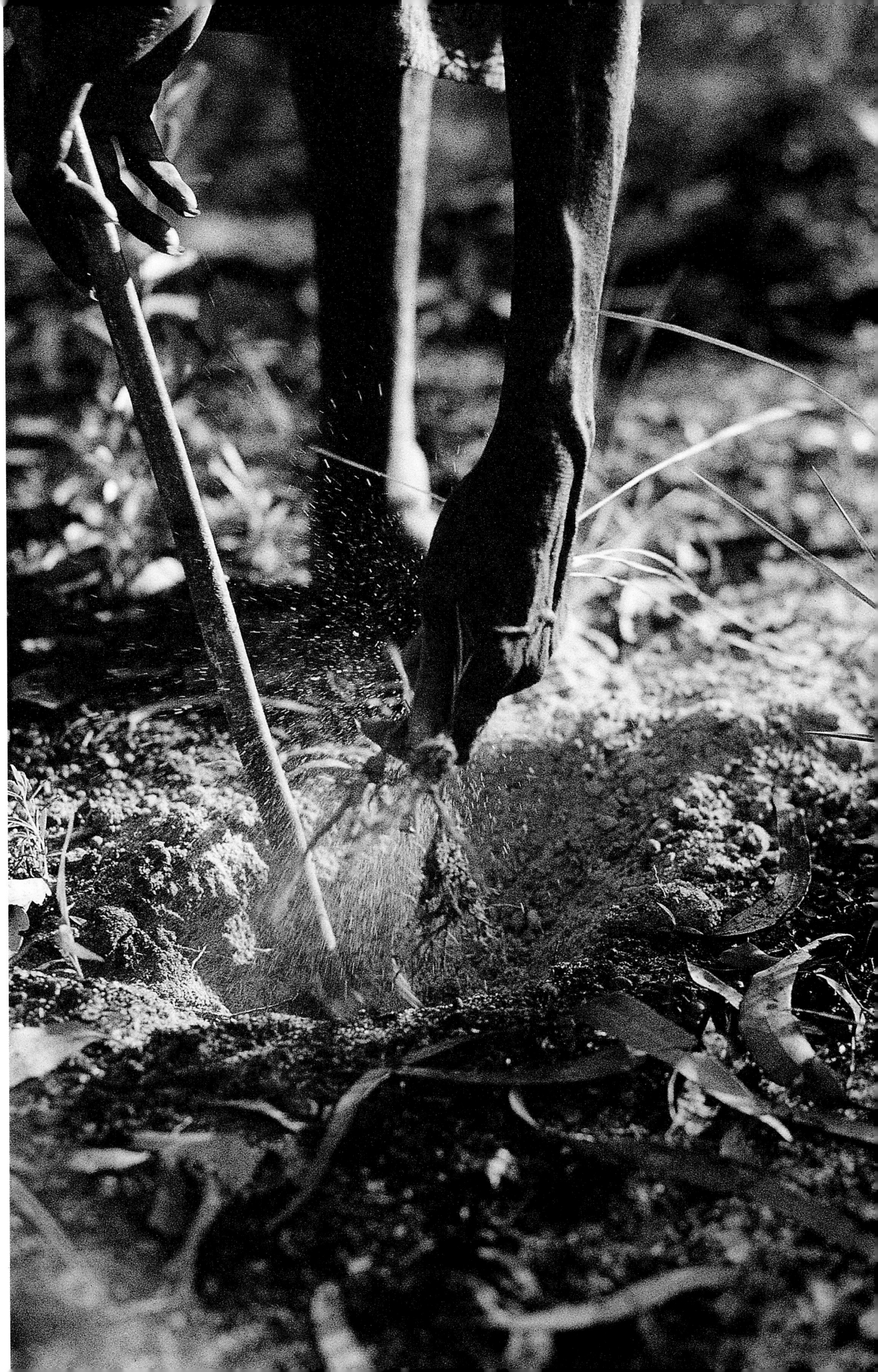

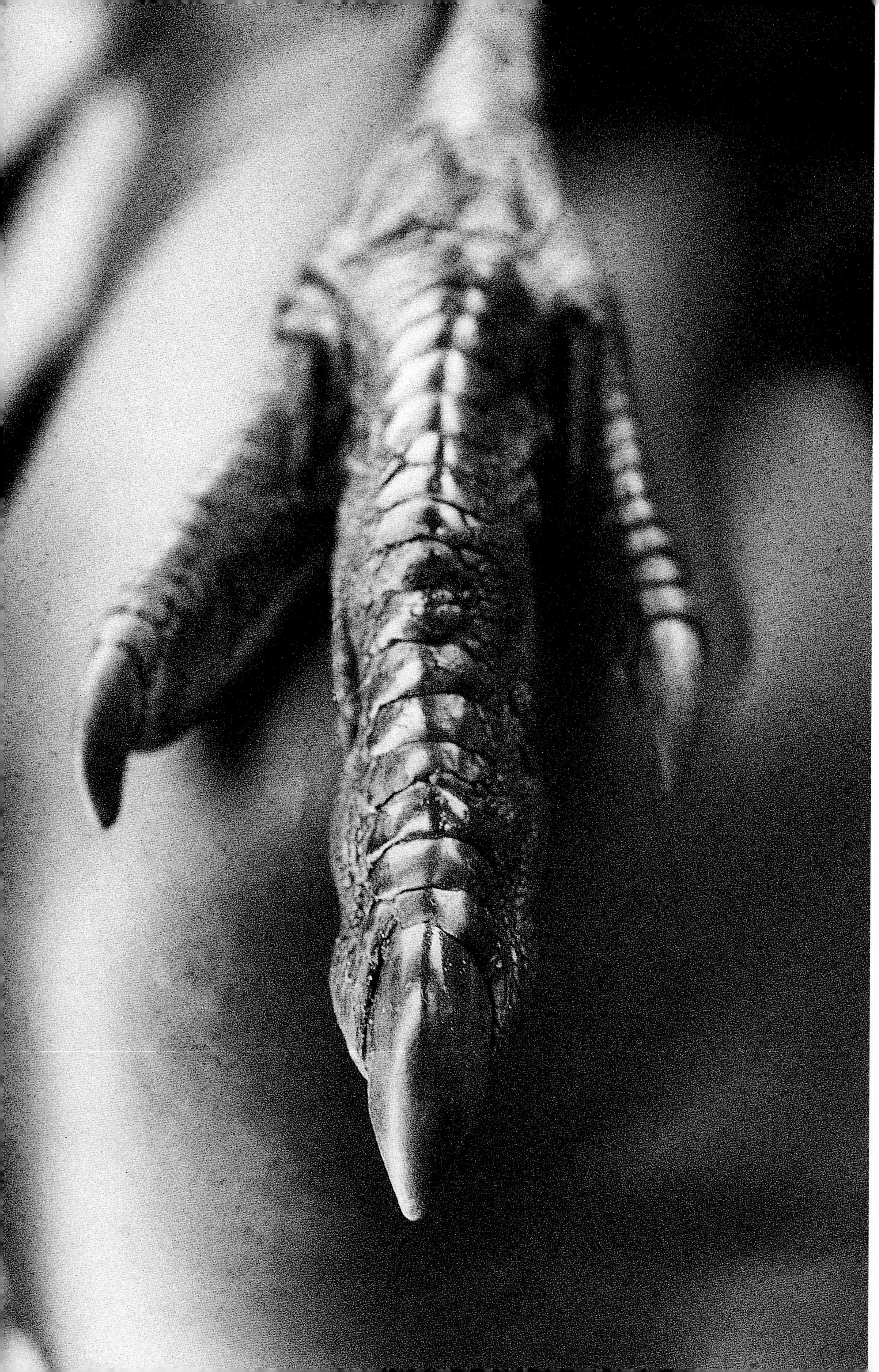

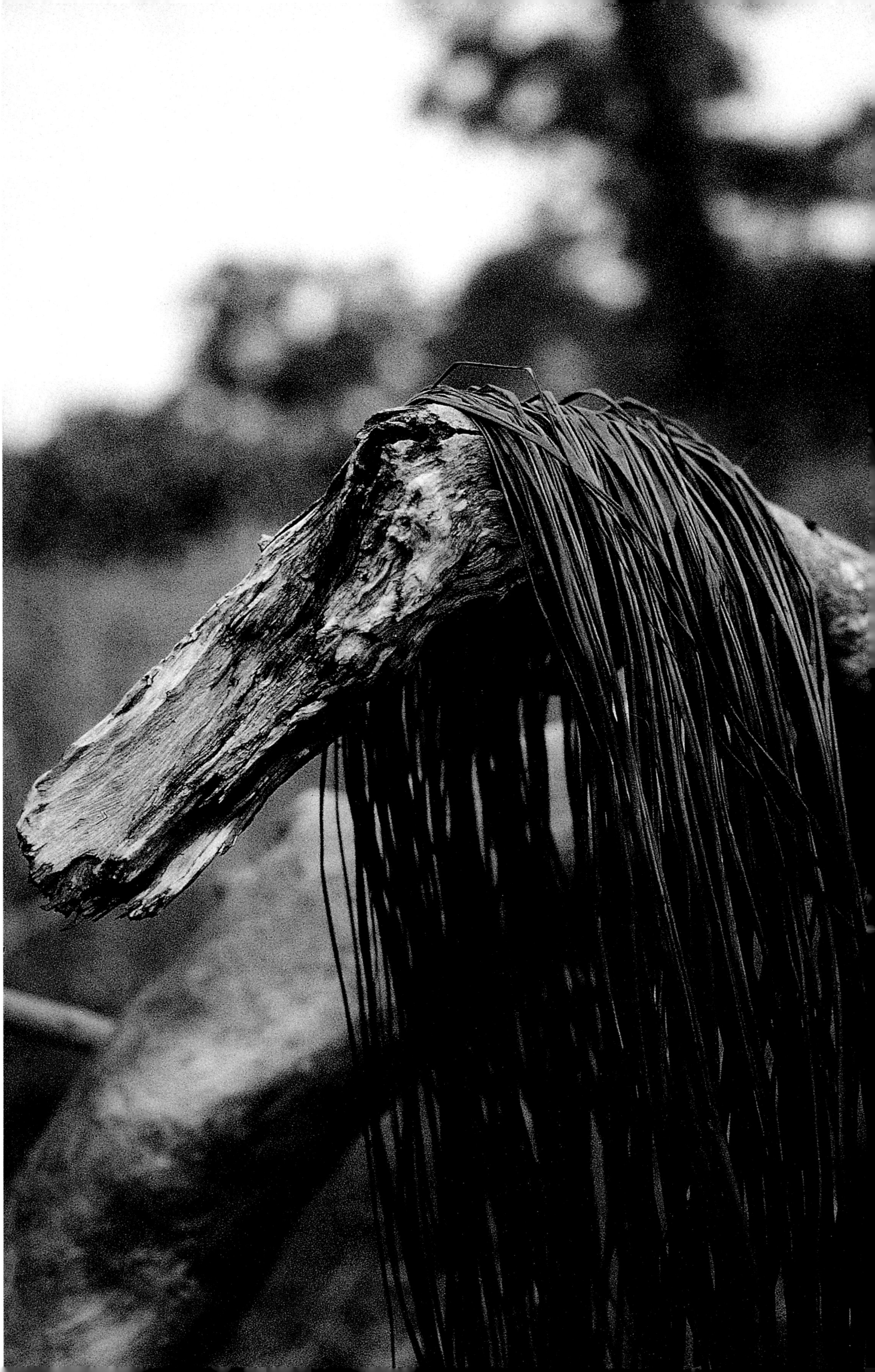

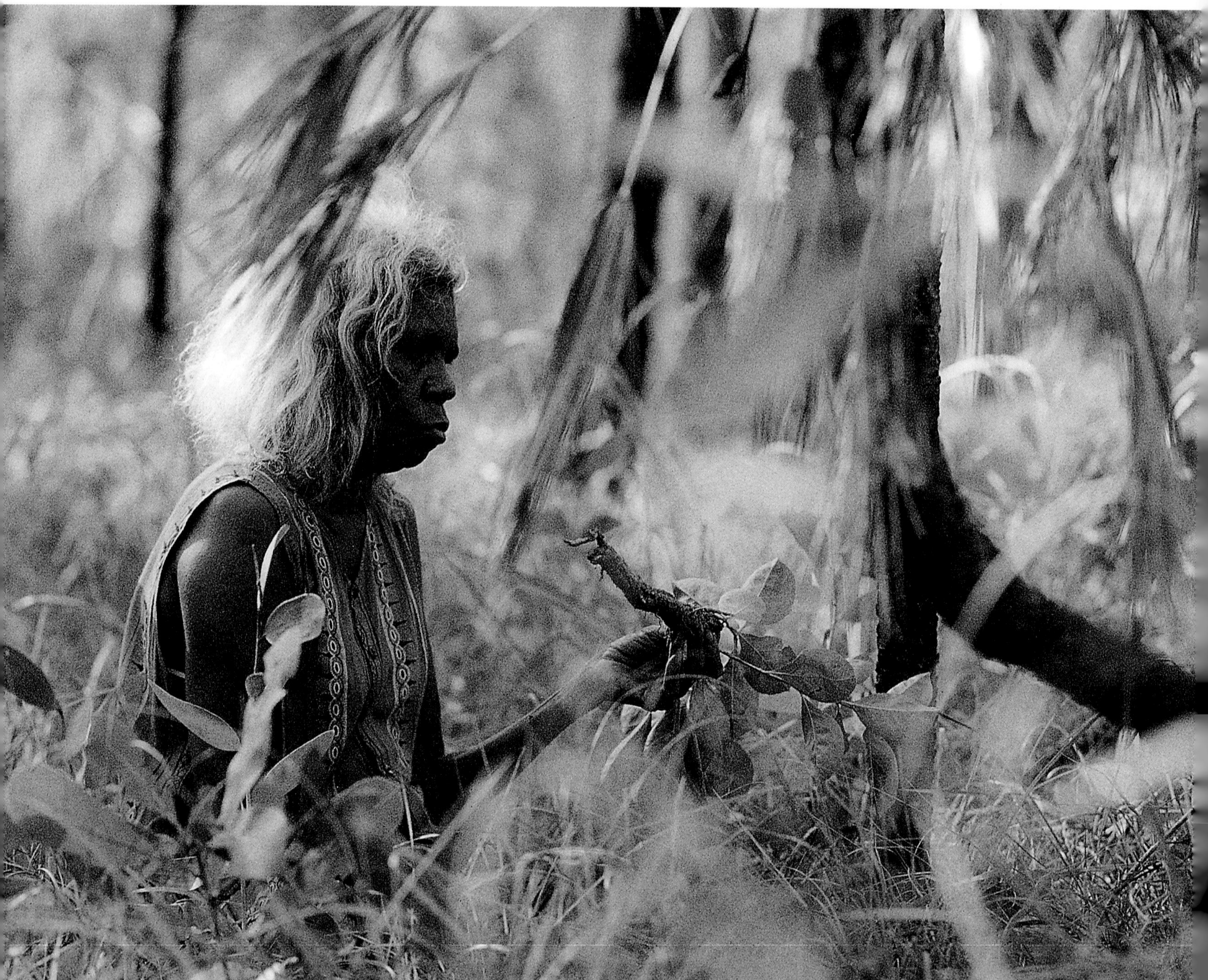

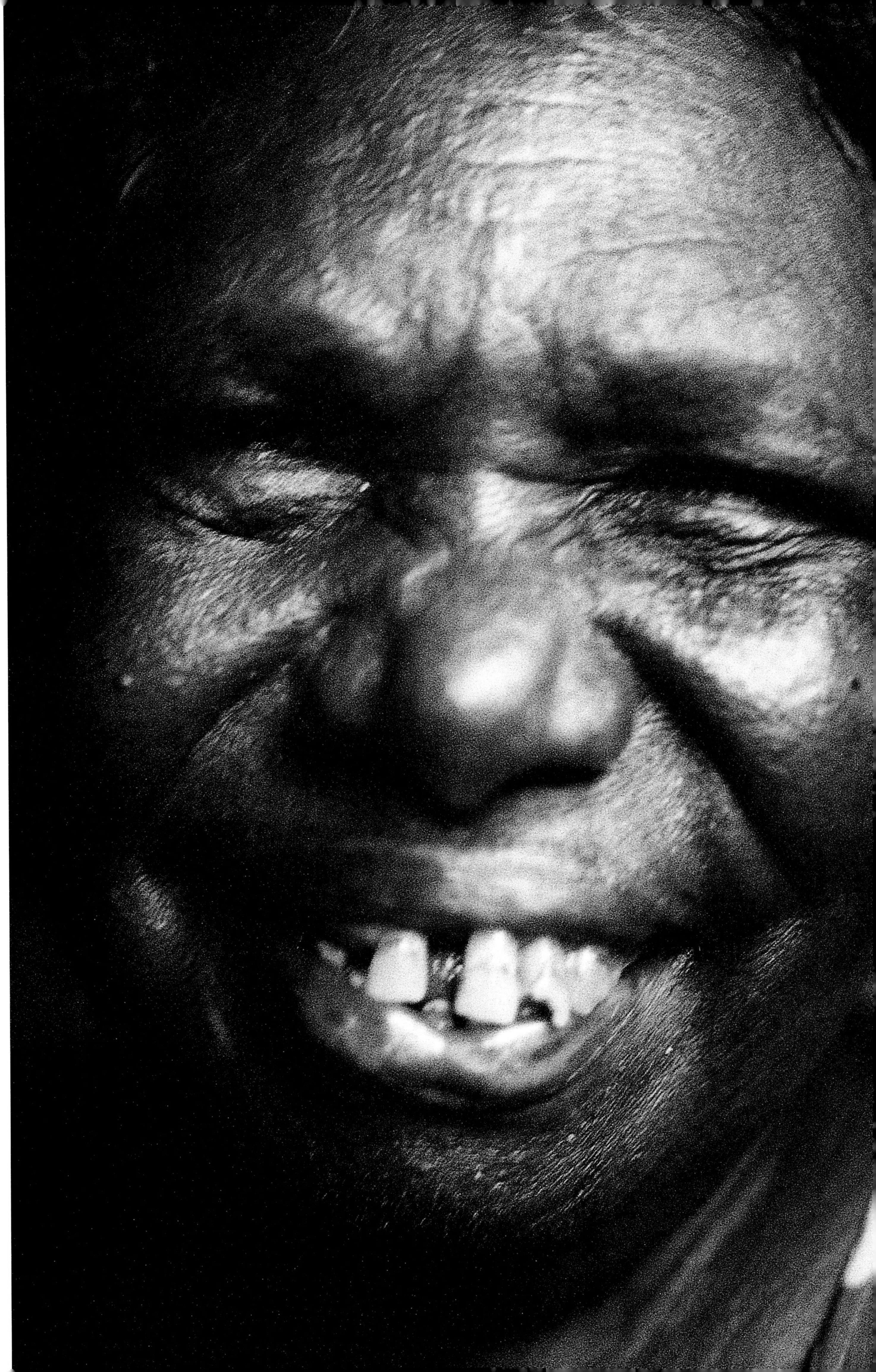

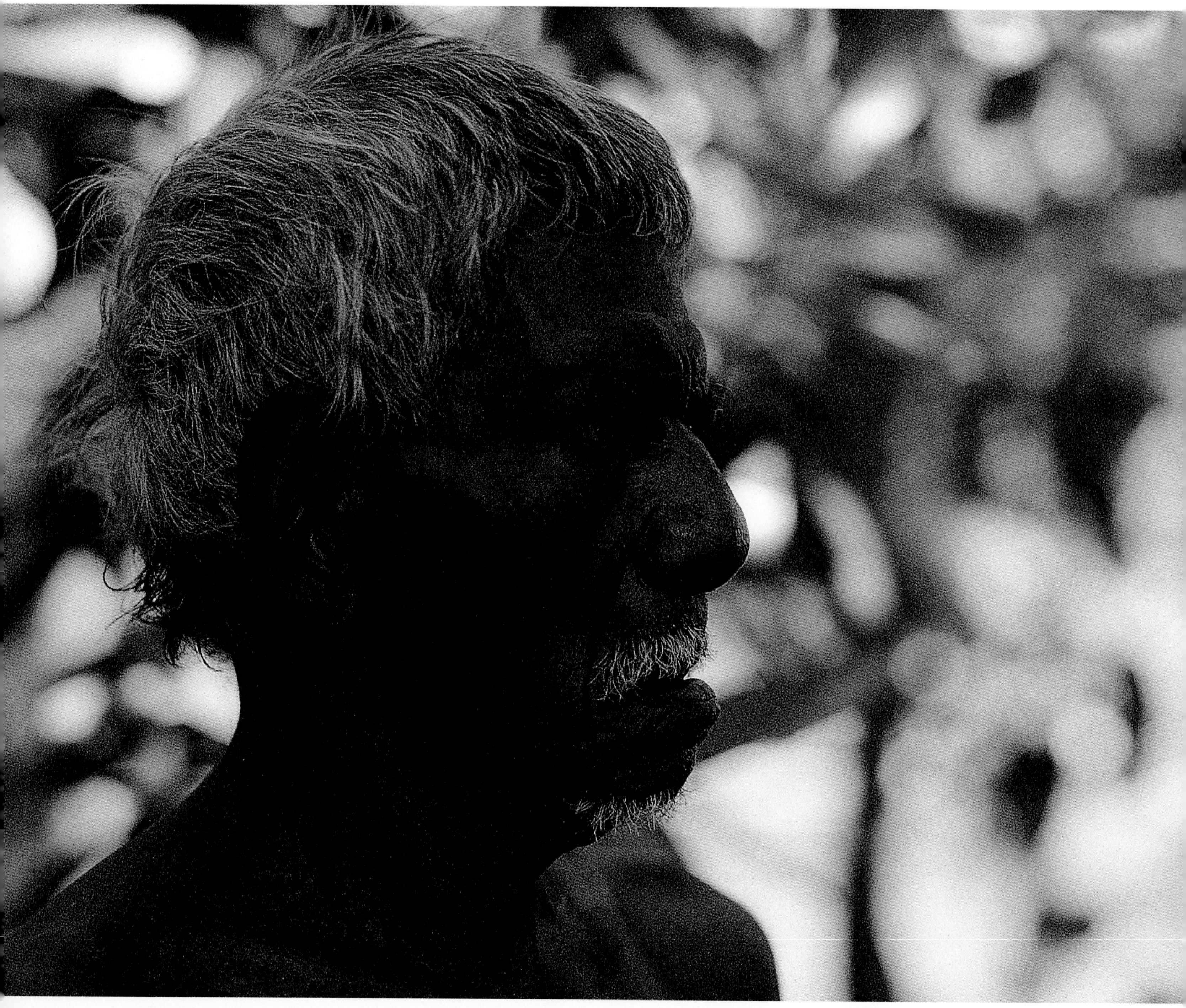

CEREMONY

Initiation – circumcision ceremony – is most important one for boys. Takes three days to one week for this ceremony. As he sits with the men and listens to the songs, he becomes more ready. Headbands and armbands are made by his grandfather – these represent the connection to the land. Painting on this boy's stomach is the cloud pattern. The old people paint on you what you are. Brother-in-law of the boy has to hold him from underneath so he can't get away.

After a circumcision ceremony, he will be taught to participate in more adult men's dances during ceremonies as he grows up. He will be taught his responsibilities from his tribal elders. This doesn't happen straightaway, as boys are around seven to twelve years old when they get circumcised. But as they get older, around fifteen to twenty, they are expected to participate more in cultural activities, whatever they may be.

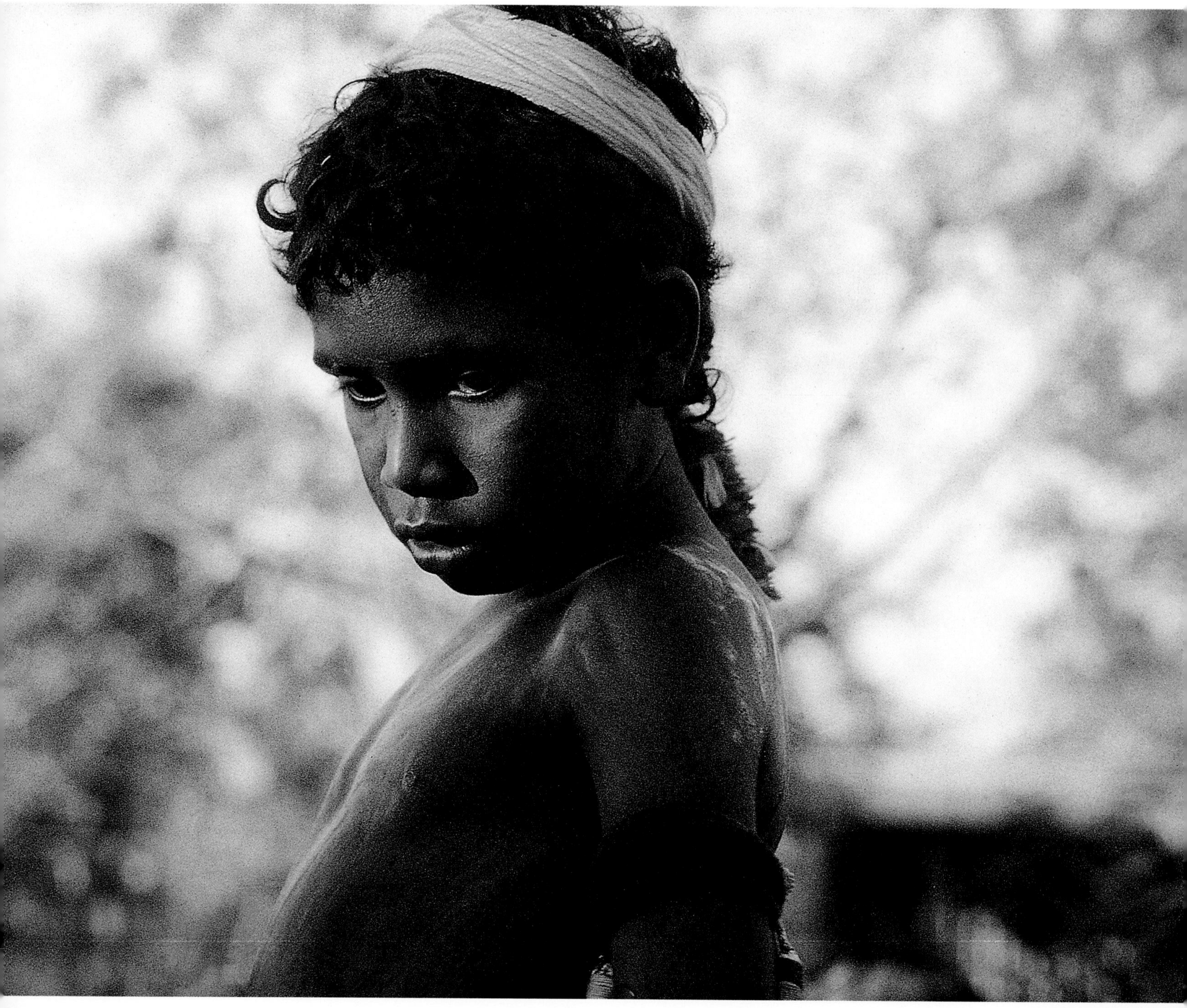

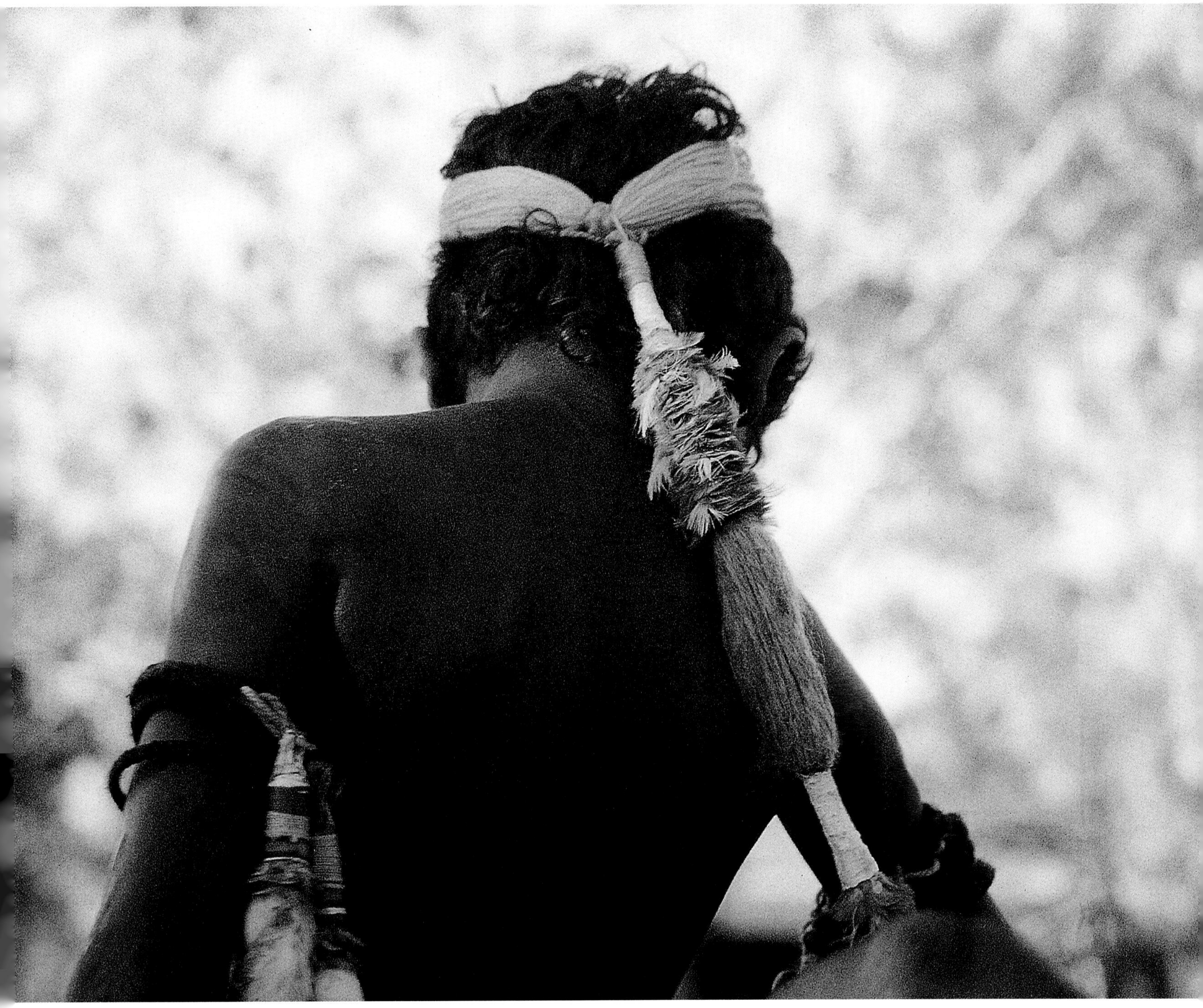

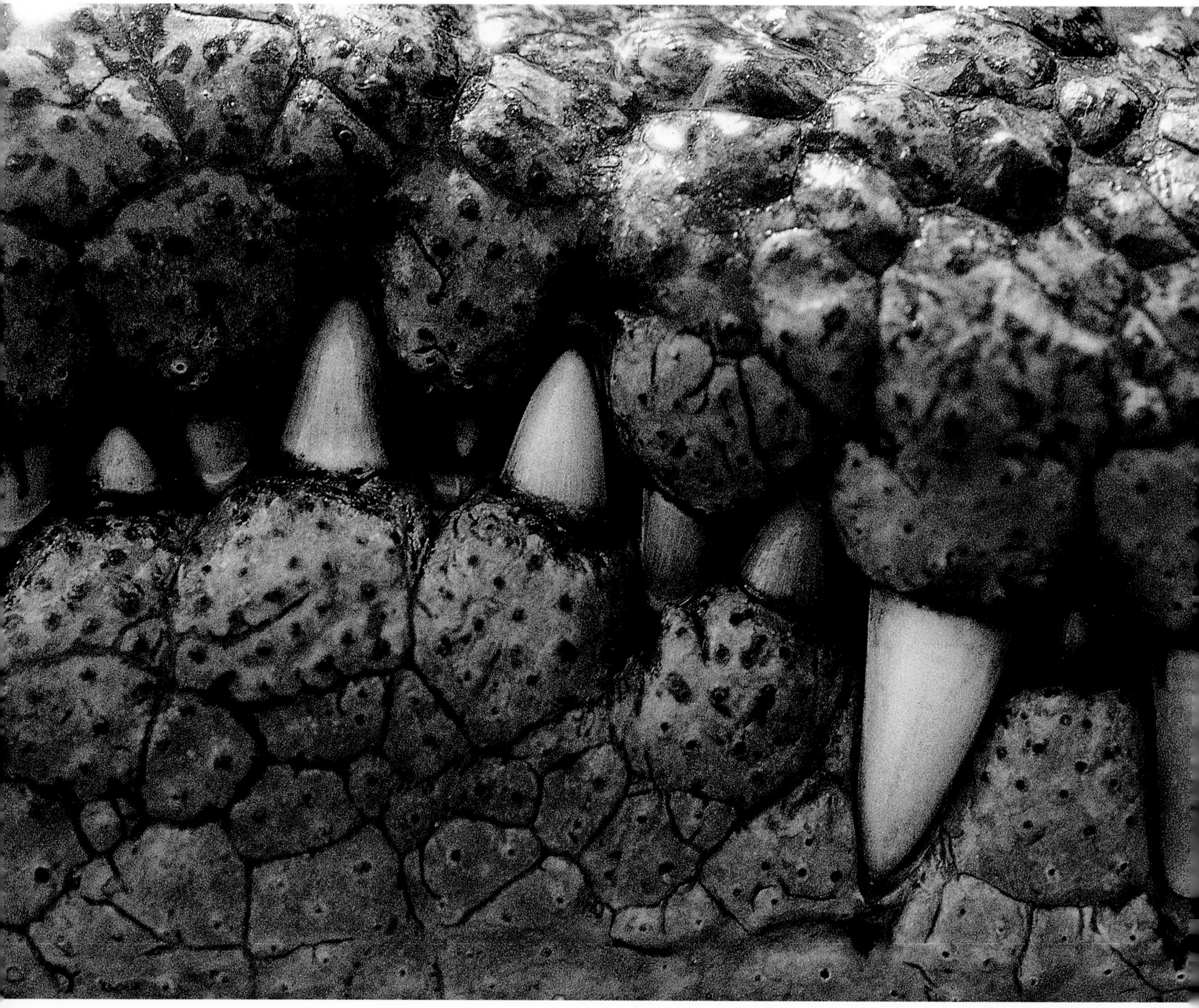

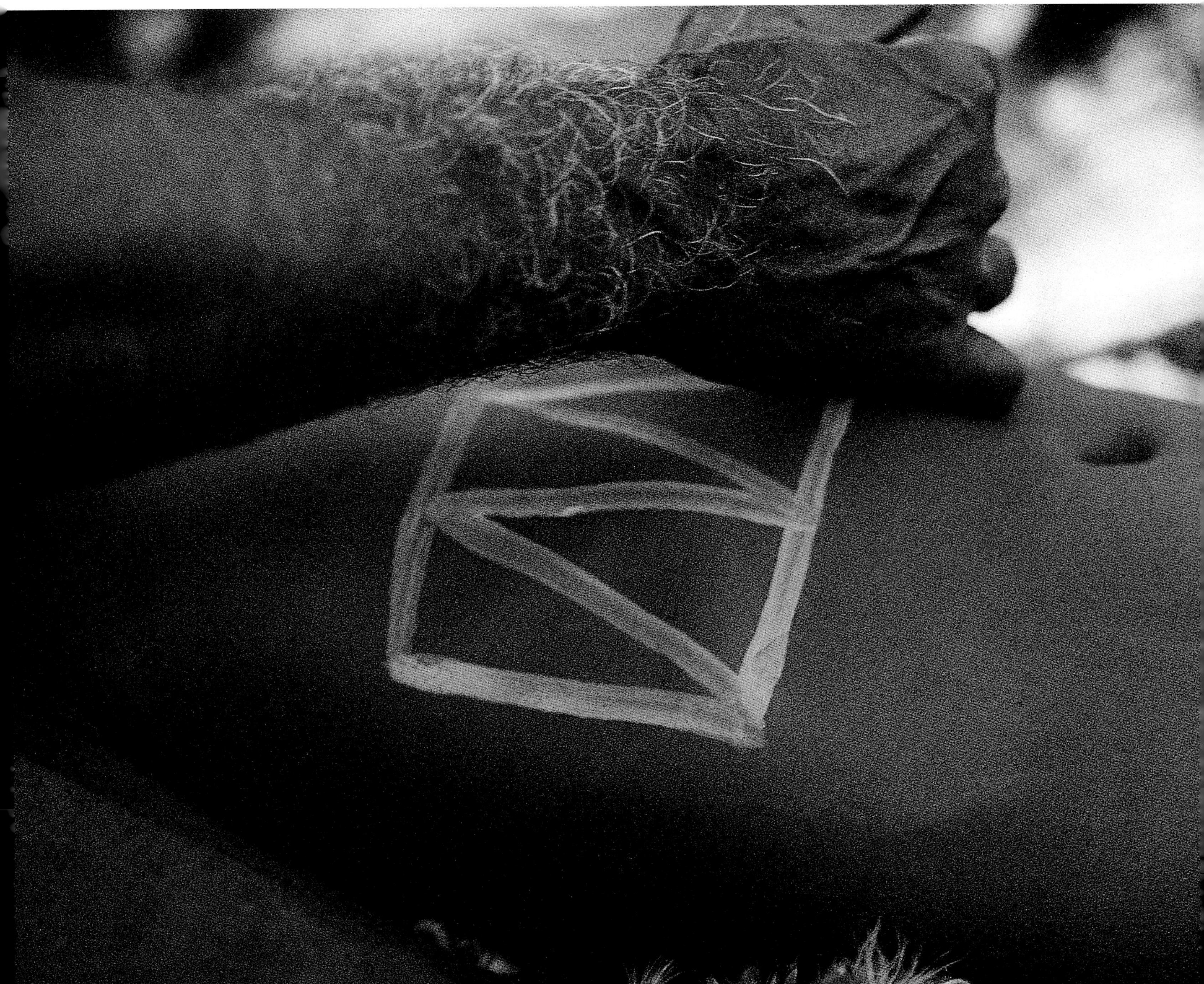

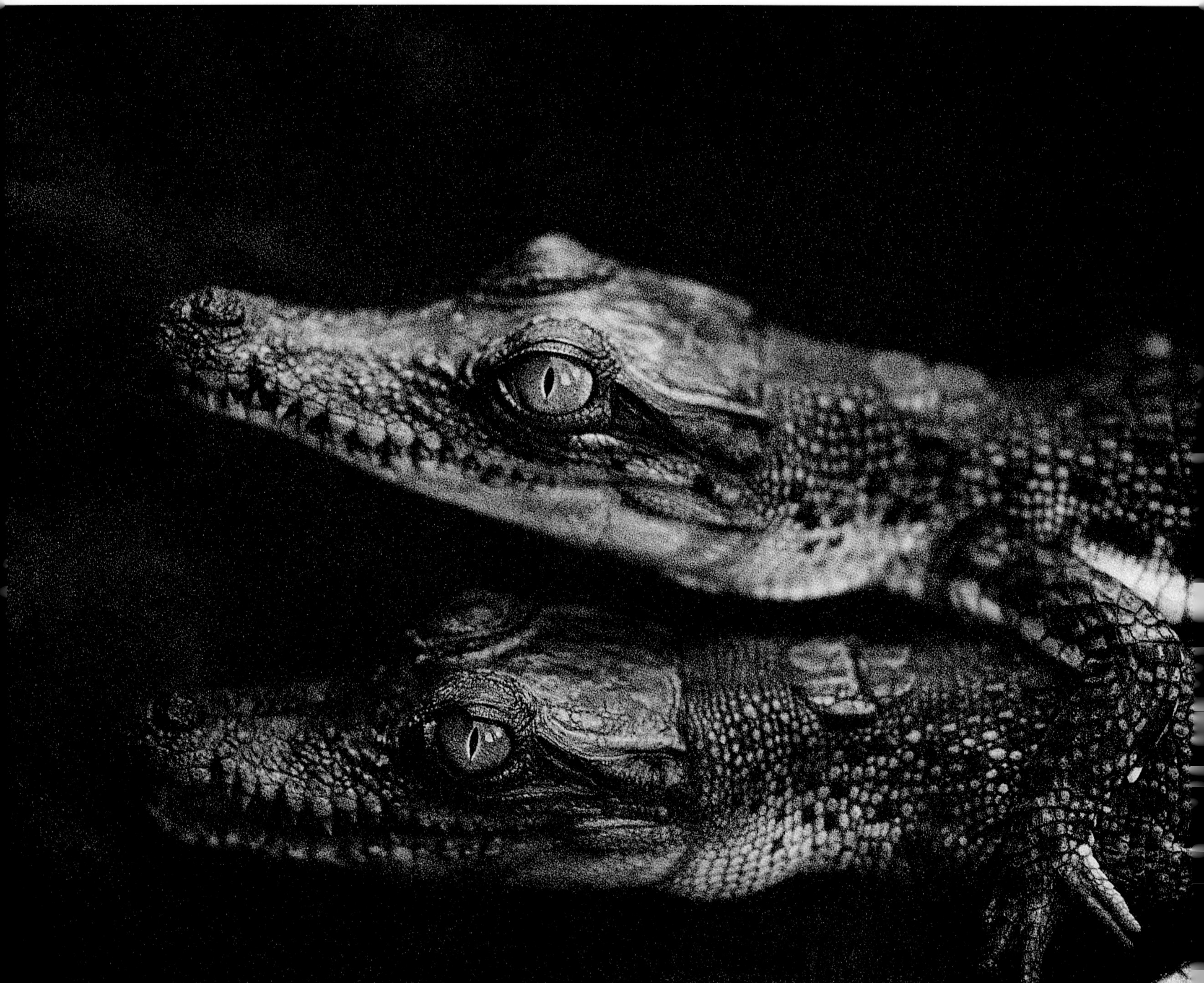

TIMELESS WOMEN

Women are more involved in everything – hunting, art and craft, dancing, gathering bush tucker, preparing it. We cook the big oysters straight on the fire, and mussels. Little oysters you can eat raw, rock oysters you can eat cooked or raw. Women are the only ones to make the strings for armbands and for sacred dillybags. Always making strings, even when doing nothing, wind it around a stick. When someone in the family needs that string they trade it for food or something. Sisters or immediate family give it to each other for free.

There's no ceremony for a girl to become a woman. Mothers use steam cleansing a few days after giving birth, this helps the woman heal and helps the baby become a strong and healthy child. When women get painted up, men aren't allowed to see them. Back in the Dreamtime, women were up there, men were followers. The women had all the stories, all the songs, then one man stole dillybags from two women and everything changed. The dillybags held all the sacred things, and when the man stole them he took away the power.

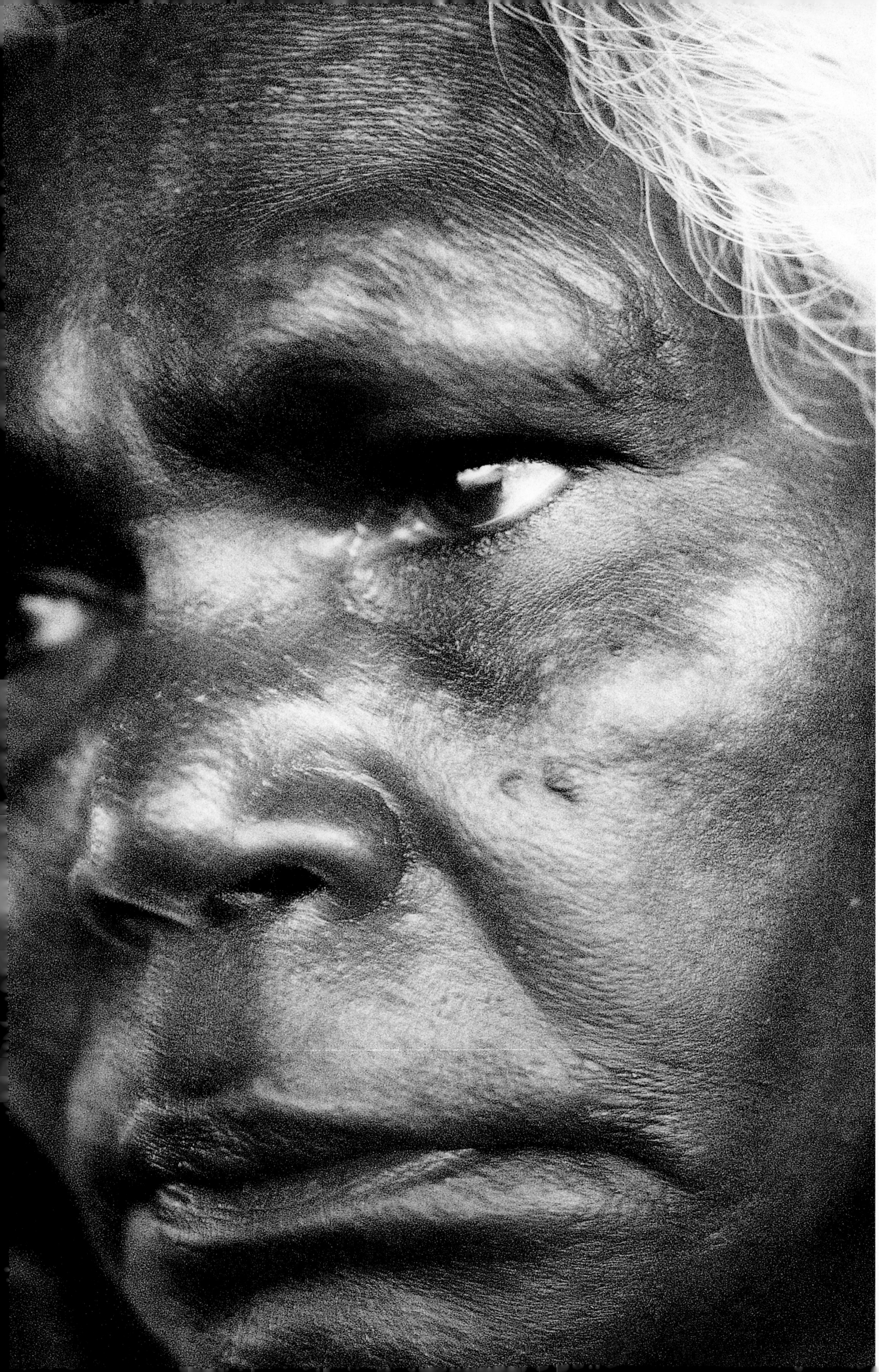

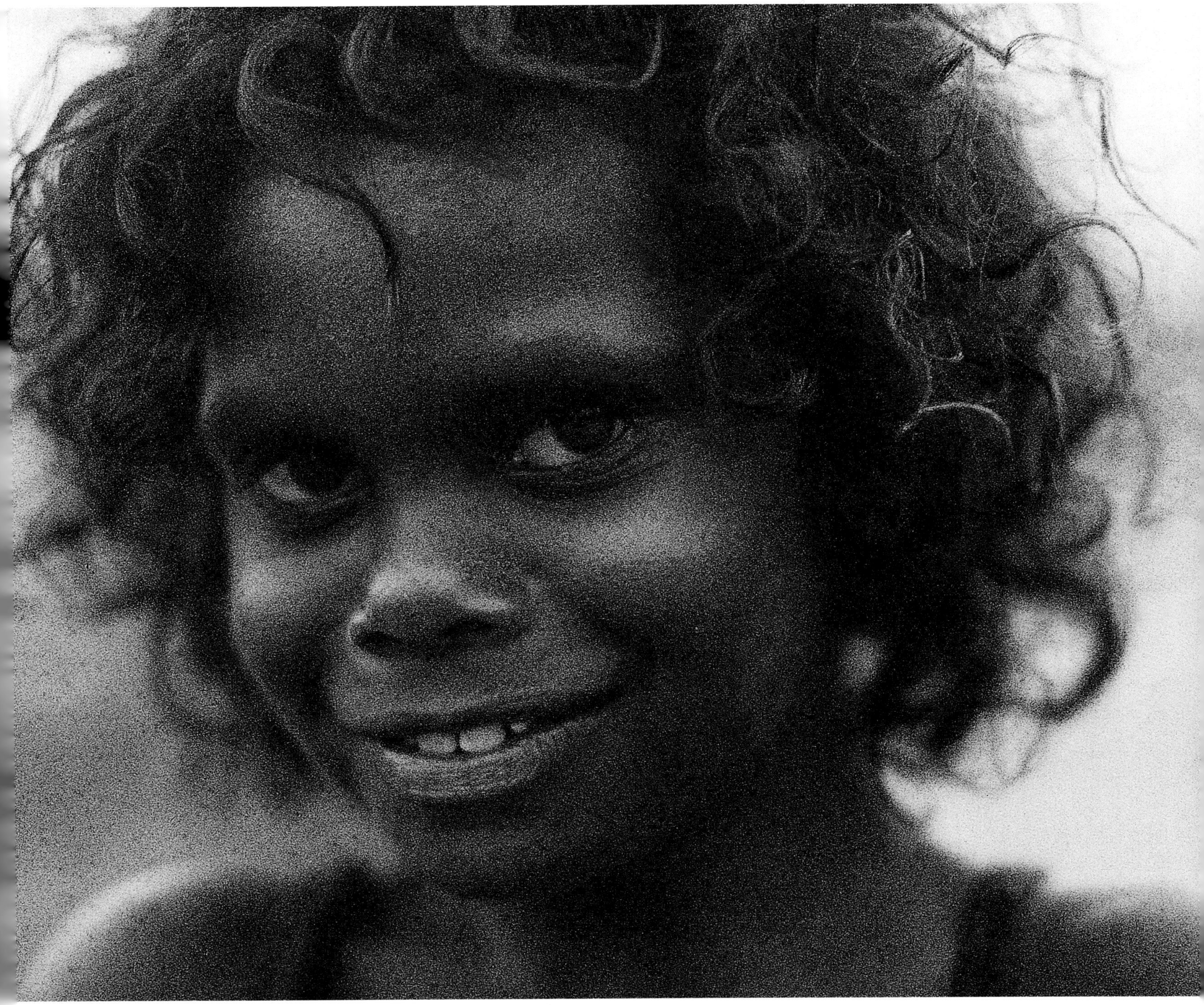

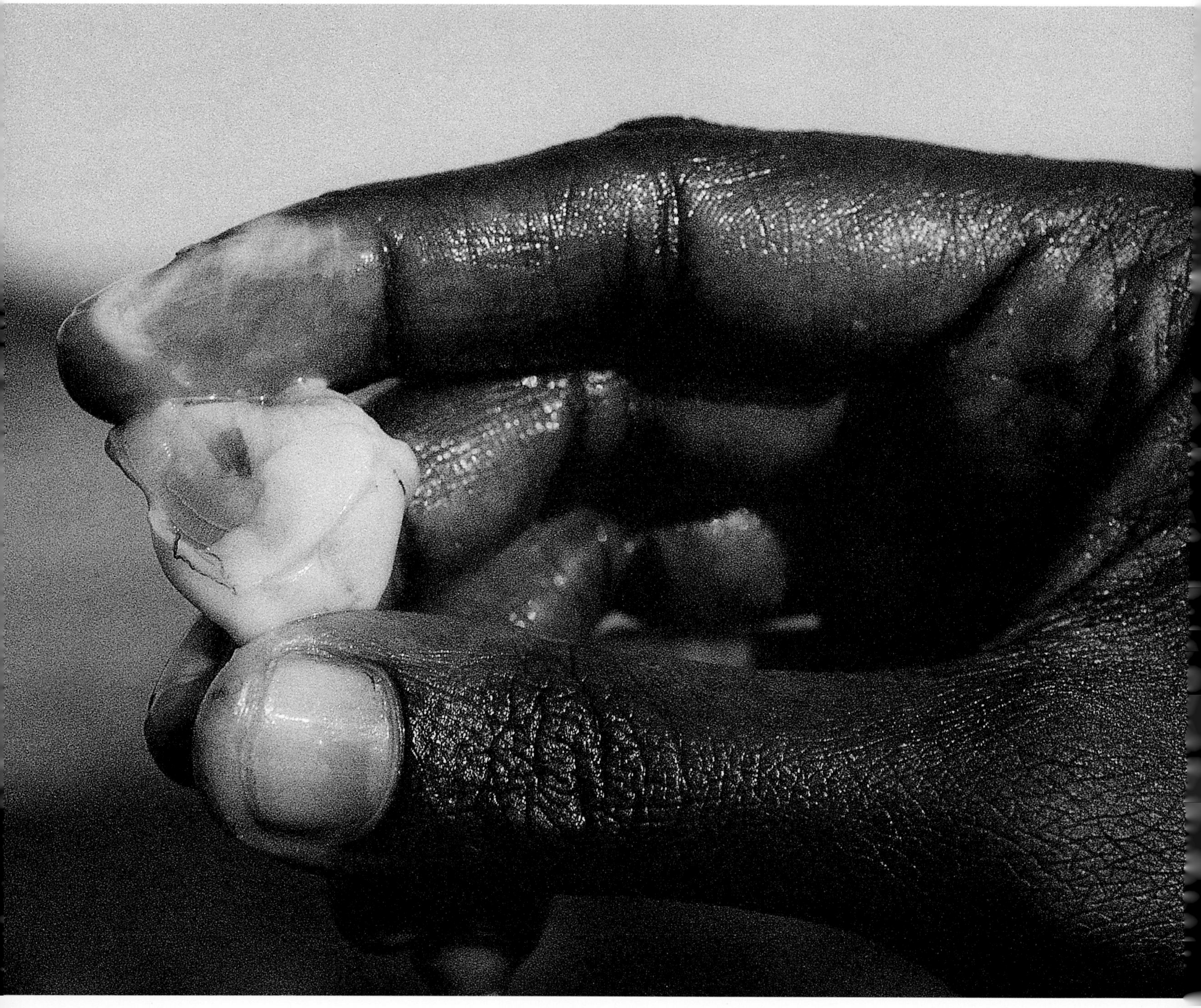

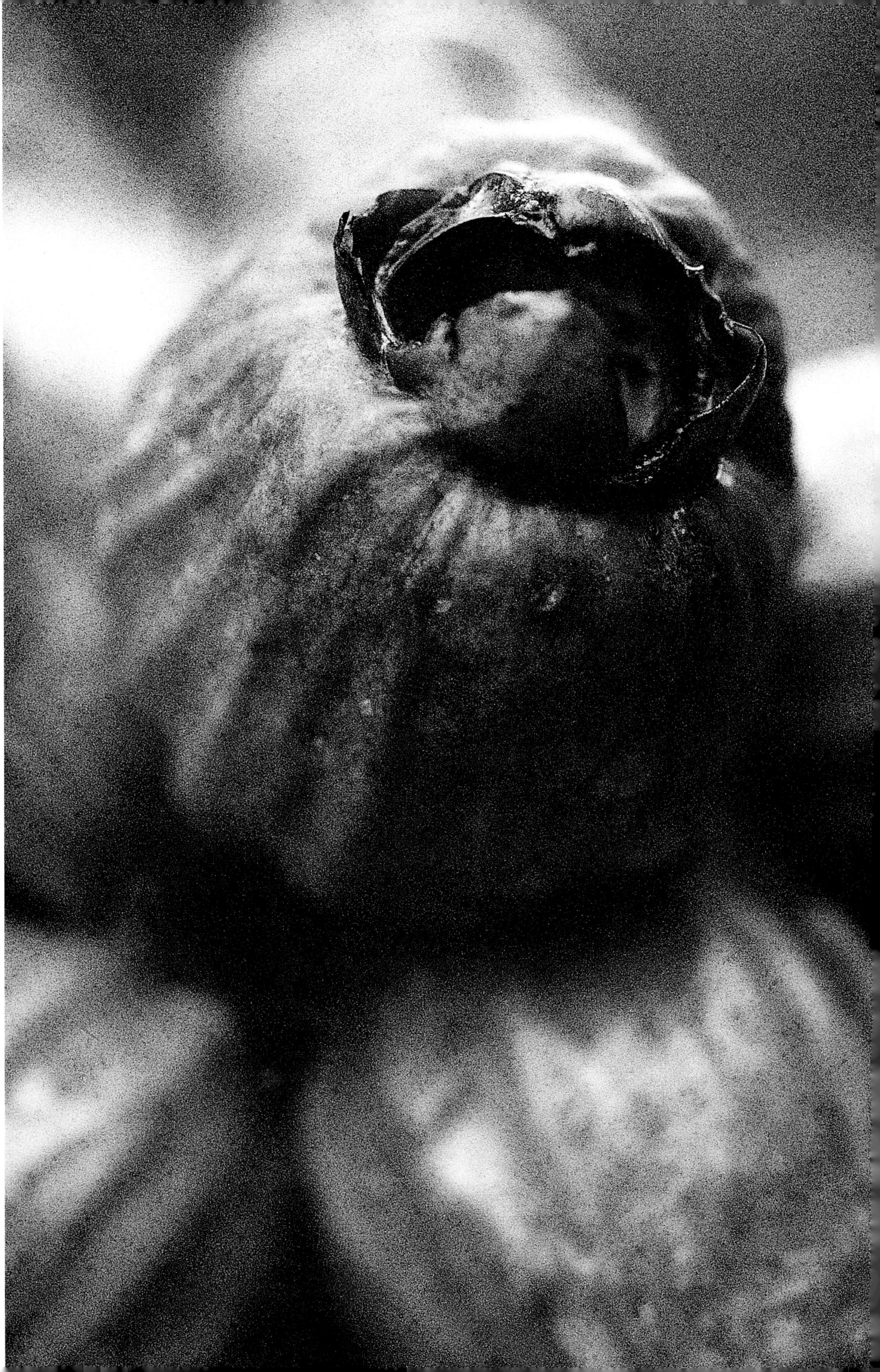

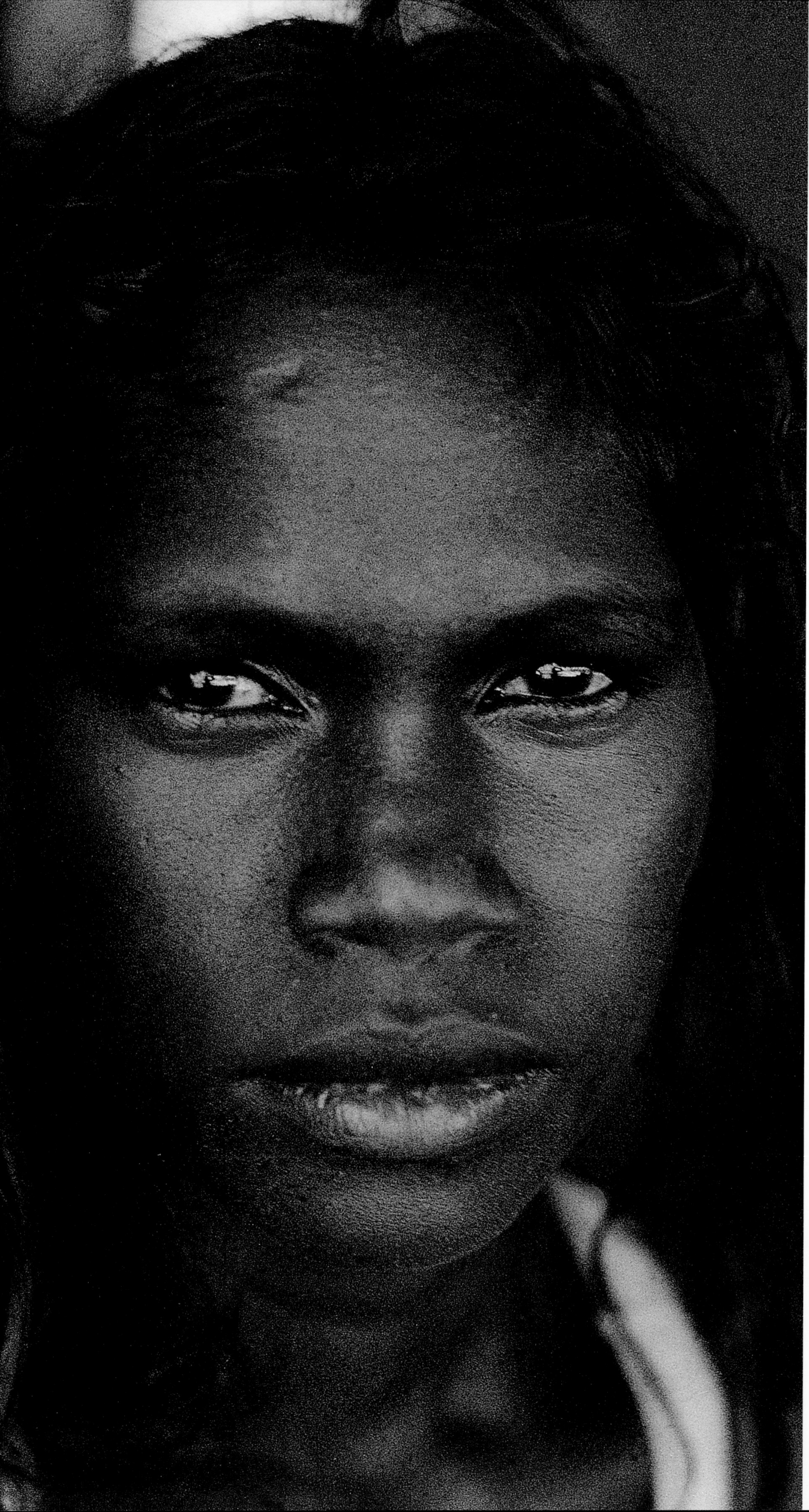

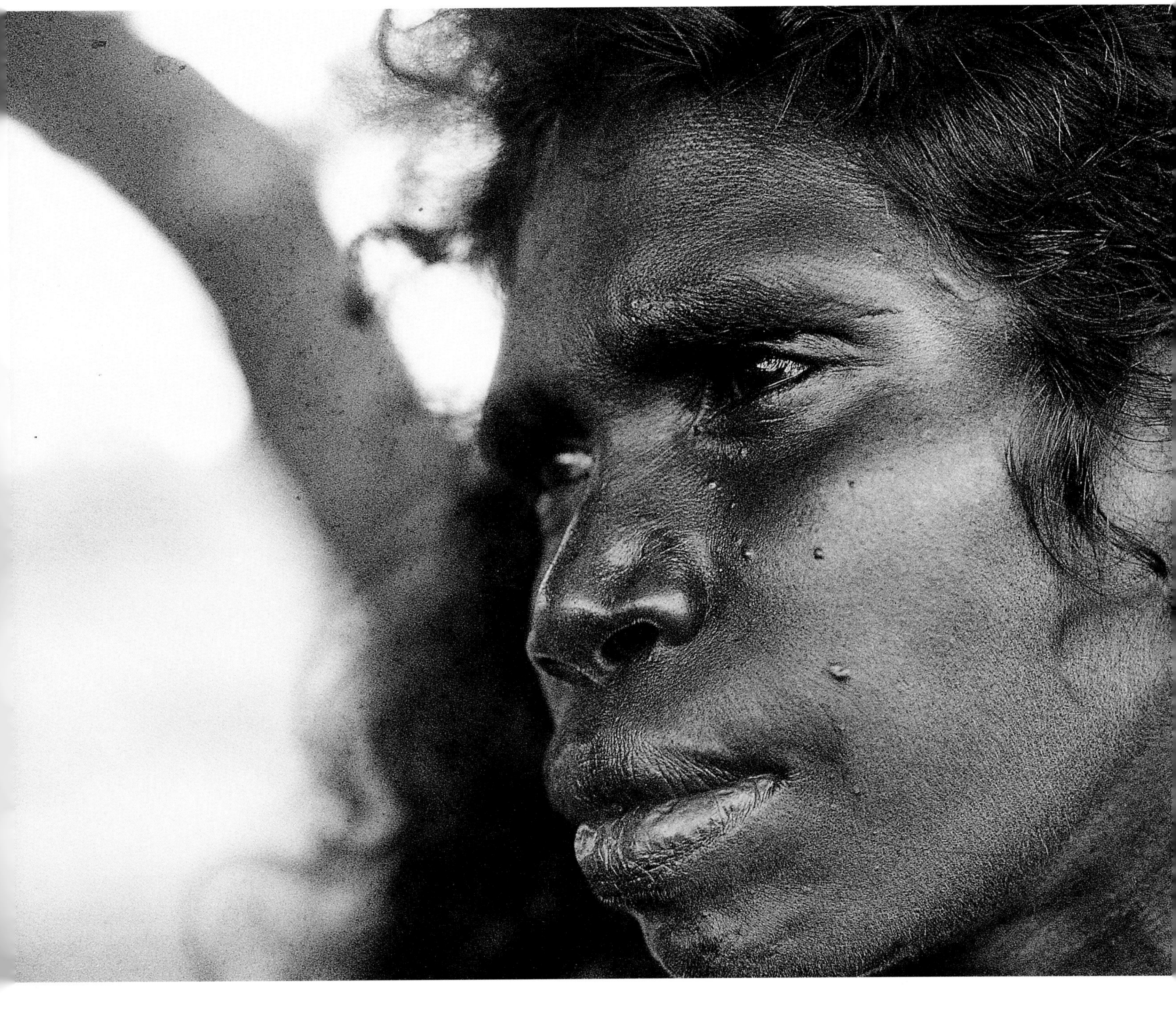

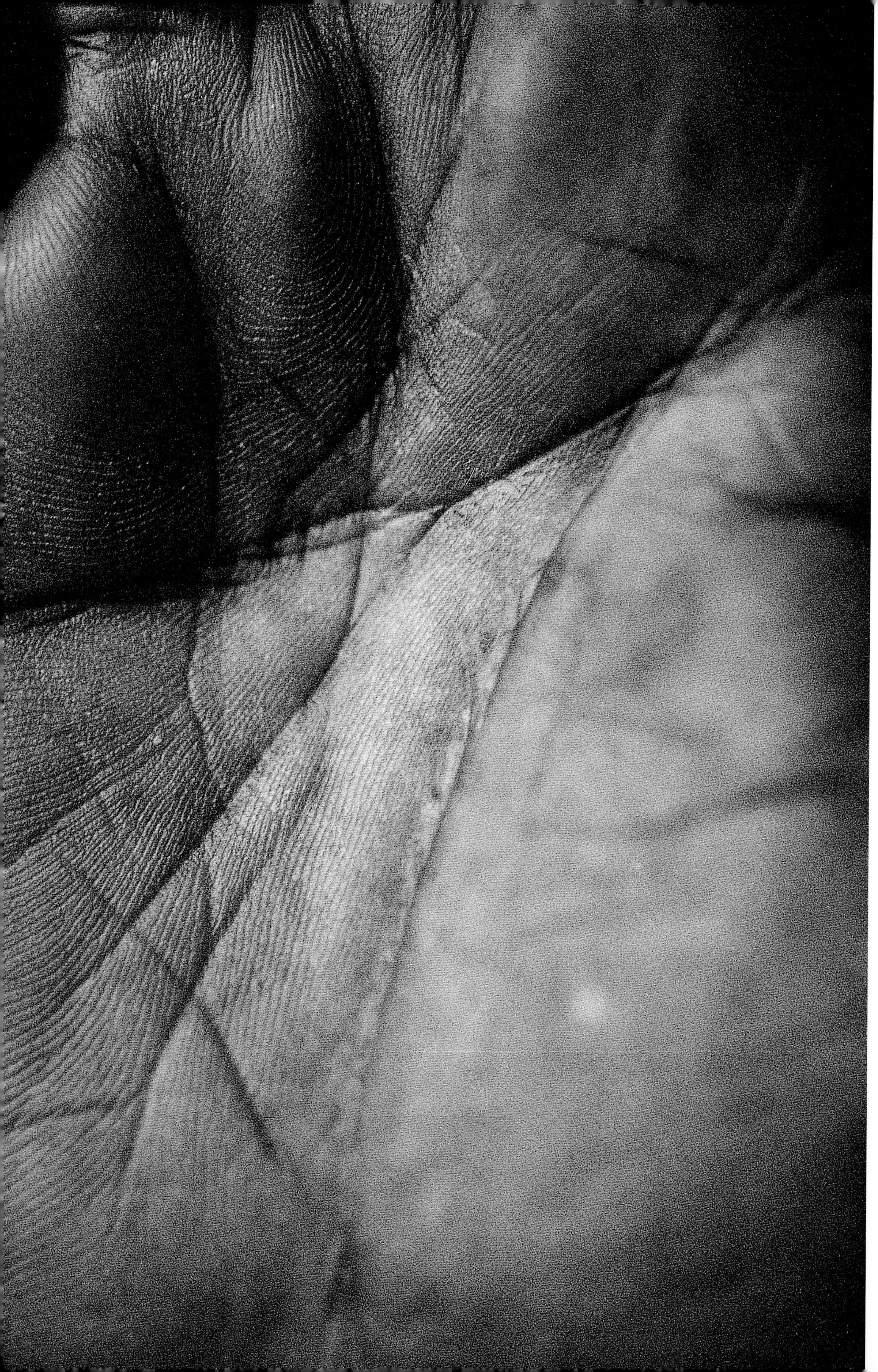

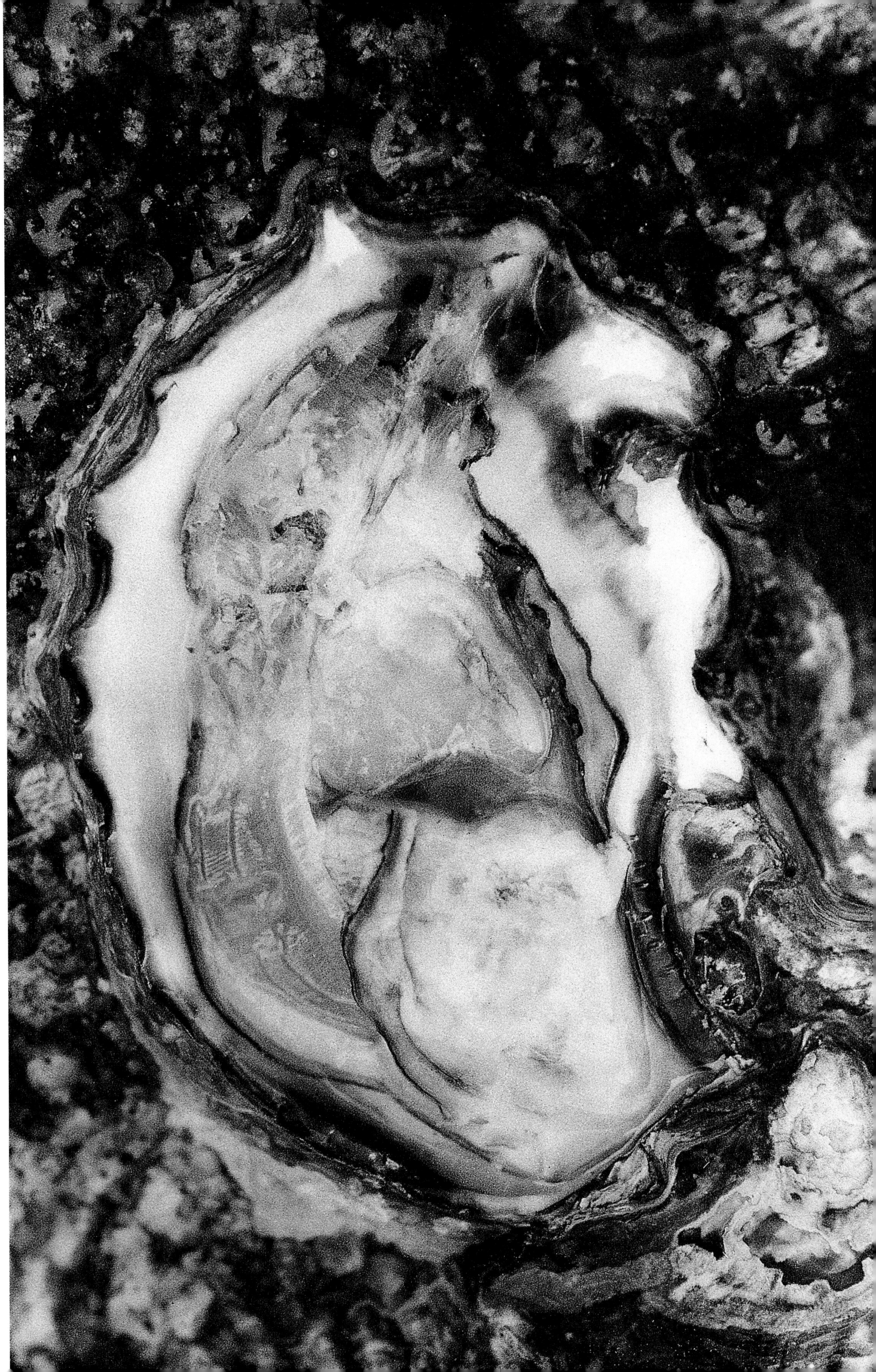

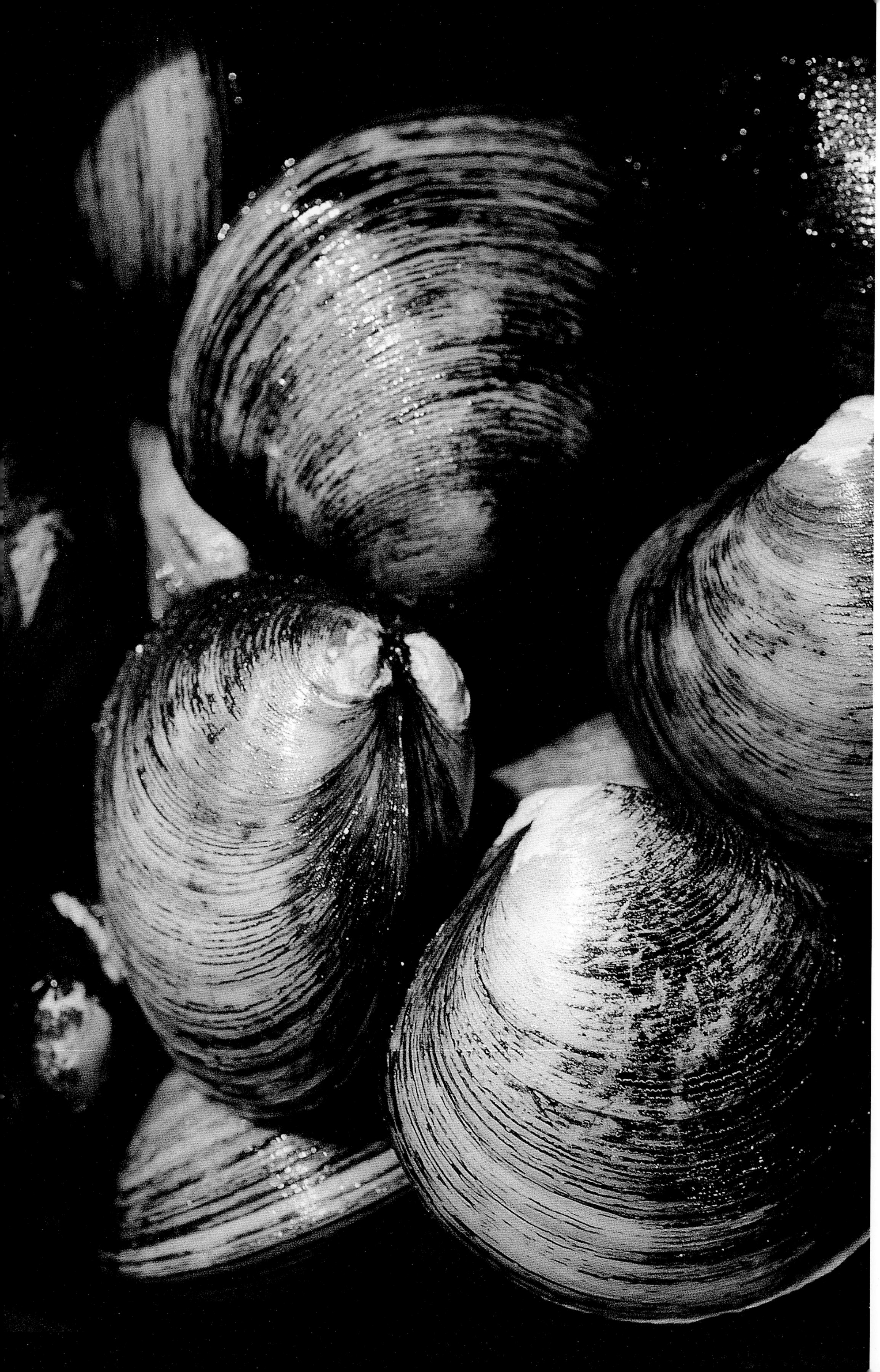

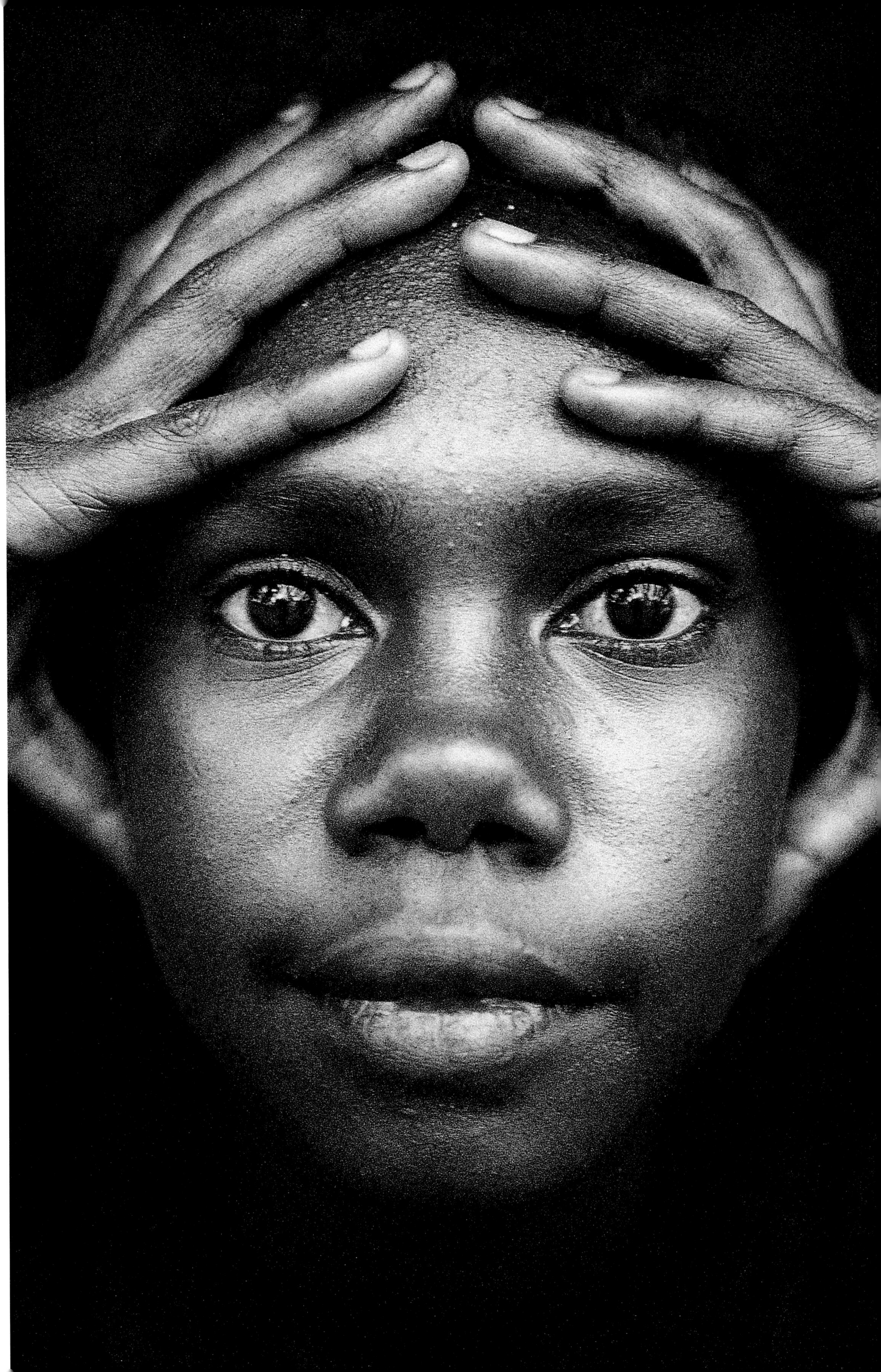

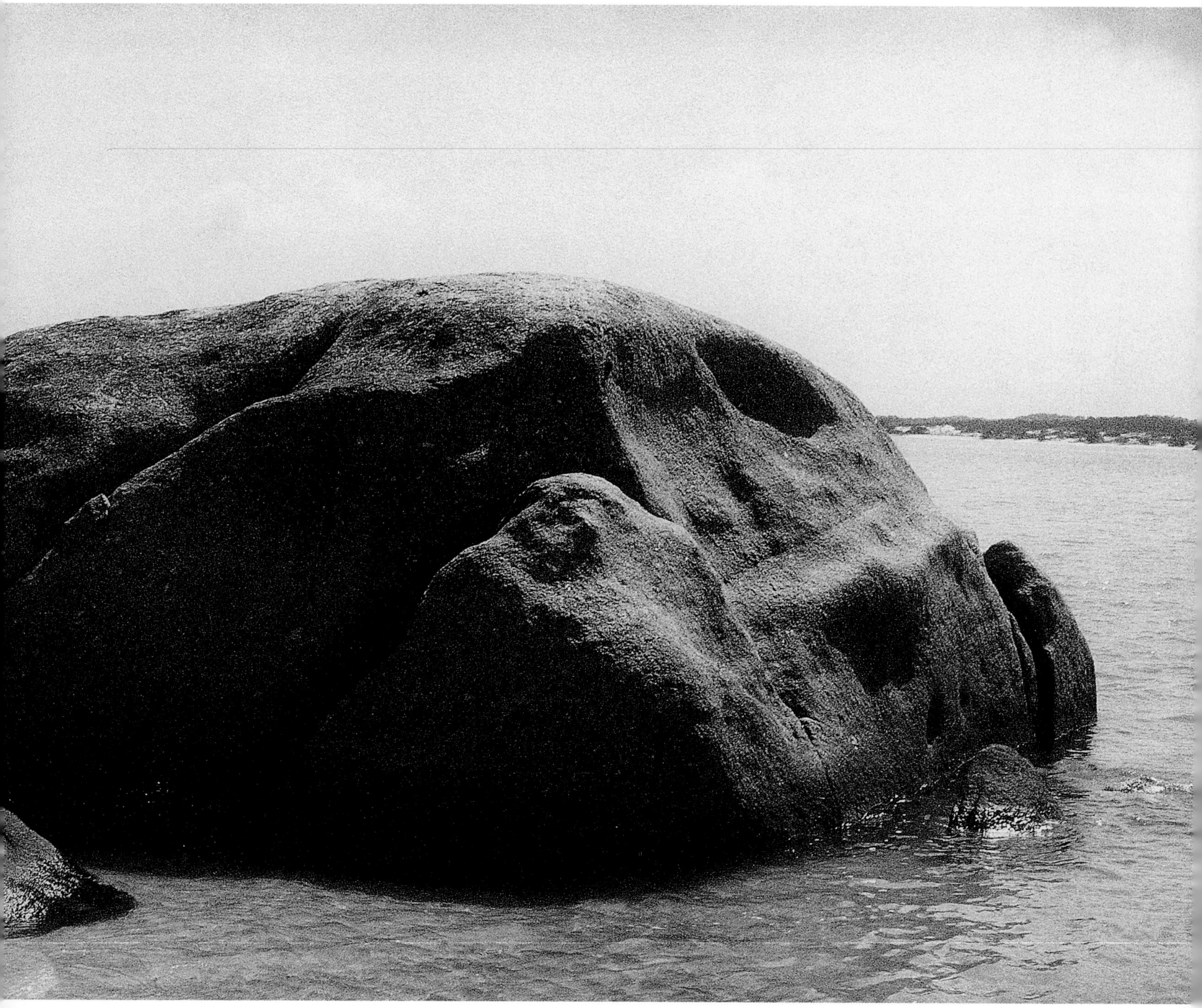

FLOWERS, STINGRAYS AND TURTLES

Stingray flower blossoms for two or three months. It grows in the forest, not on the beach. When the plant blossoms it shows that it is a good time to eat the gäpirri, the spotted stingray. The Yolngu people only eat the spotted stingray then. There are other flowers for other stingrays. Spotted stingray is the Gumatj people's totem. The liver of the stingray is best. We cut the barb away because it is dangerous.

The big sea turtle is number one on the menu. It feeds maybe three or four families, you're very popular when you catch one! Male turtles are stronger. Females are sometimes heavier; if she's got the eggs, it slows her down. Turtle neck goes to the skipper, turtle heart goes to the one who spears it. Turtle eggs are great for when you're thirsty and there are no creeks or waterholes, then you eat them raw. You can eat them both ways, raw or cooked. Eggs are found by sticking a stick in the sand. If it comes up with yolk, you've found eggs. Sometimes you search for hours because the turtle makes a fake nest and tricks you.

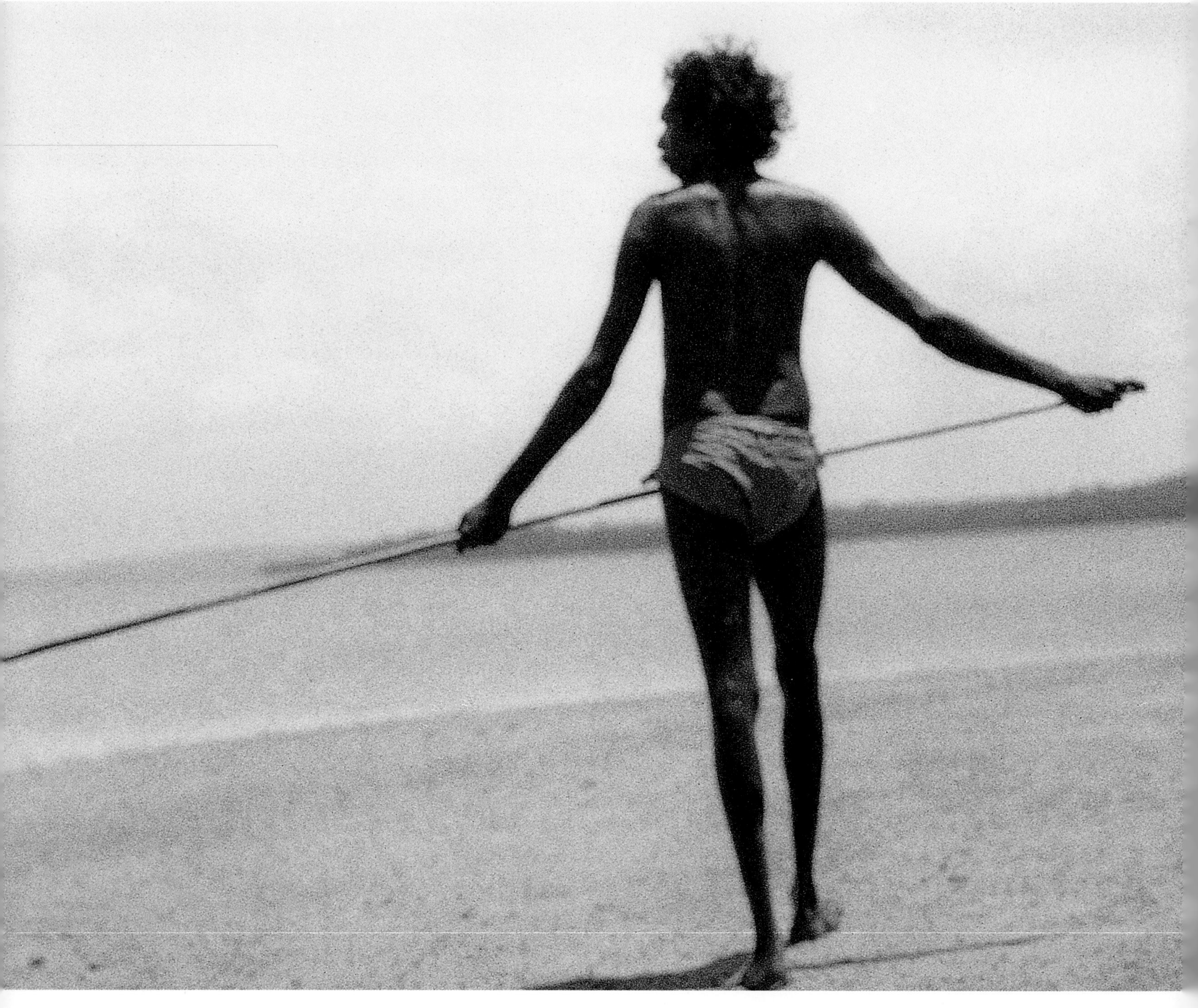

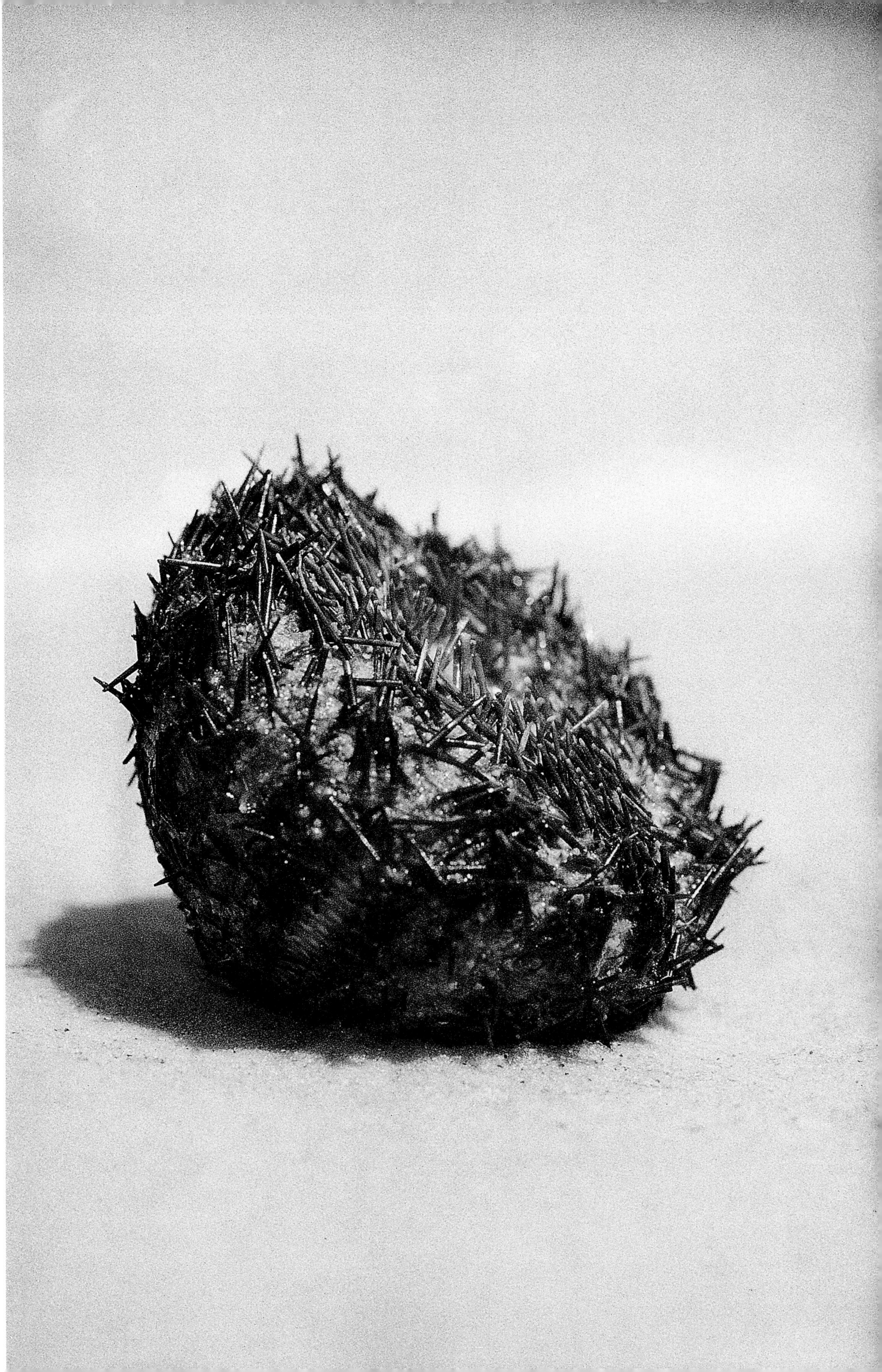

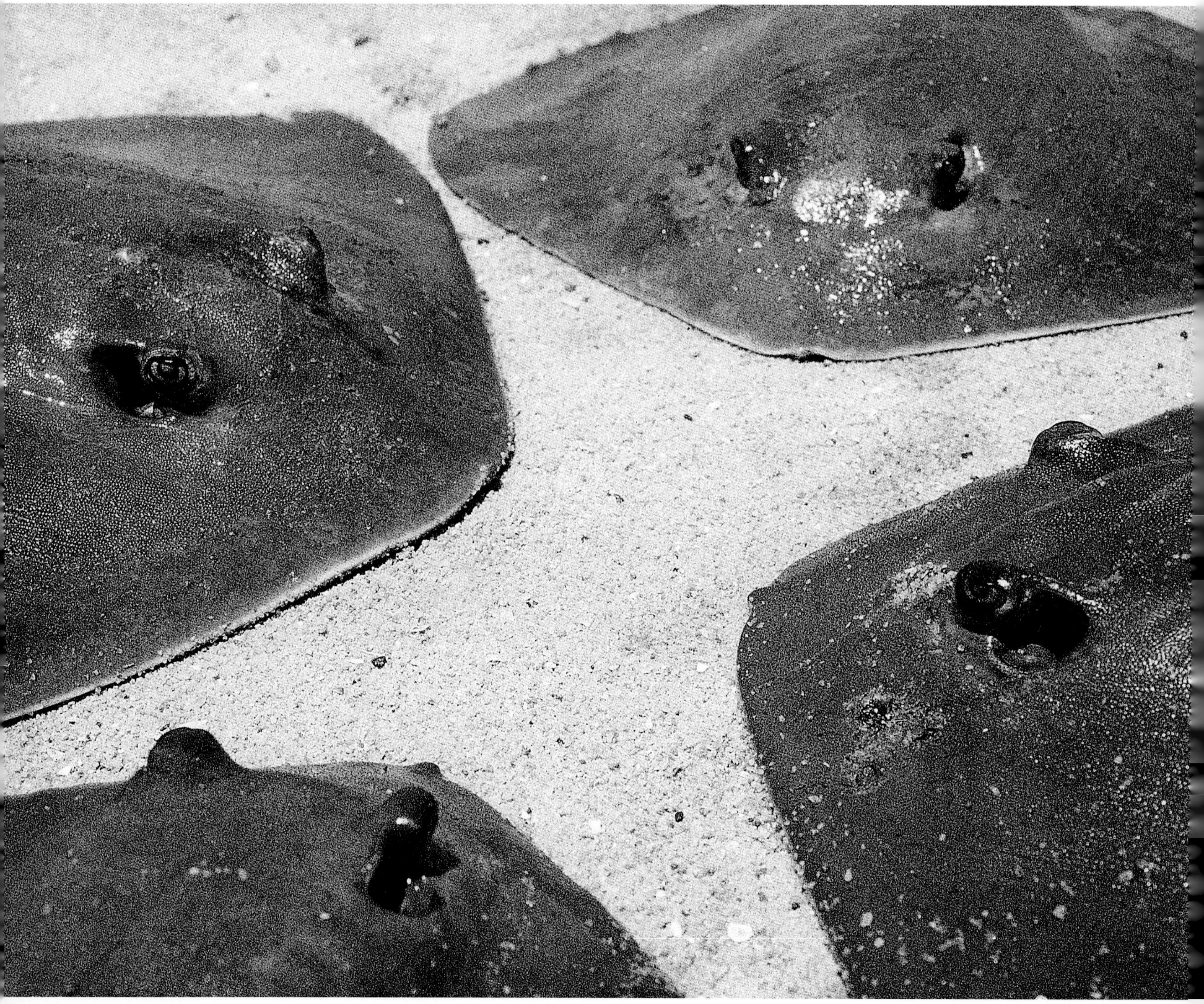

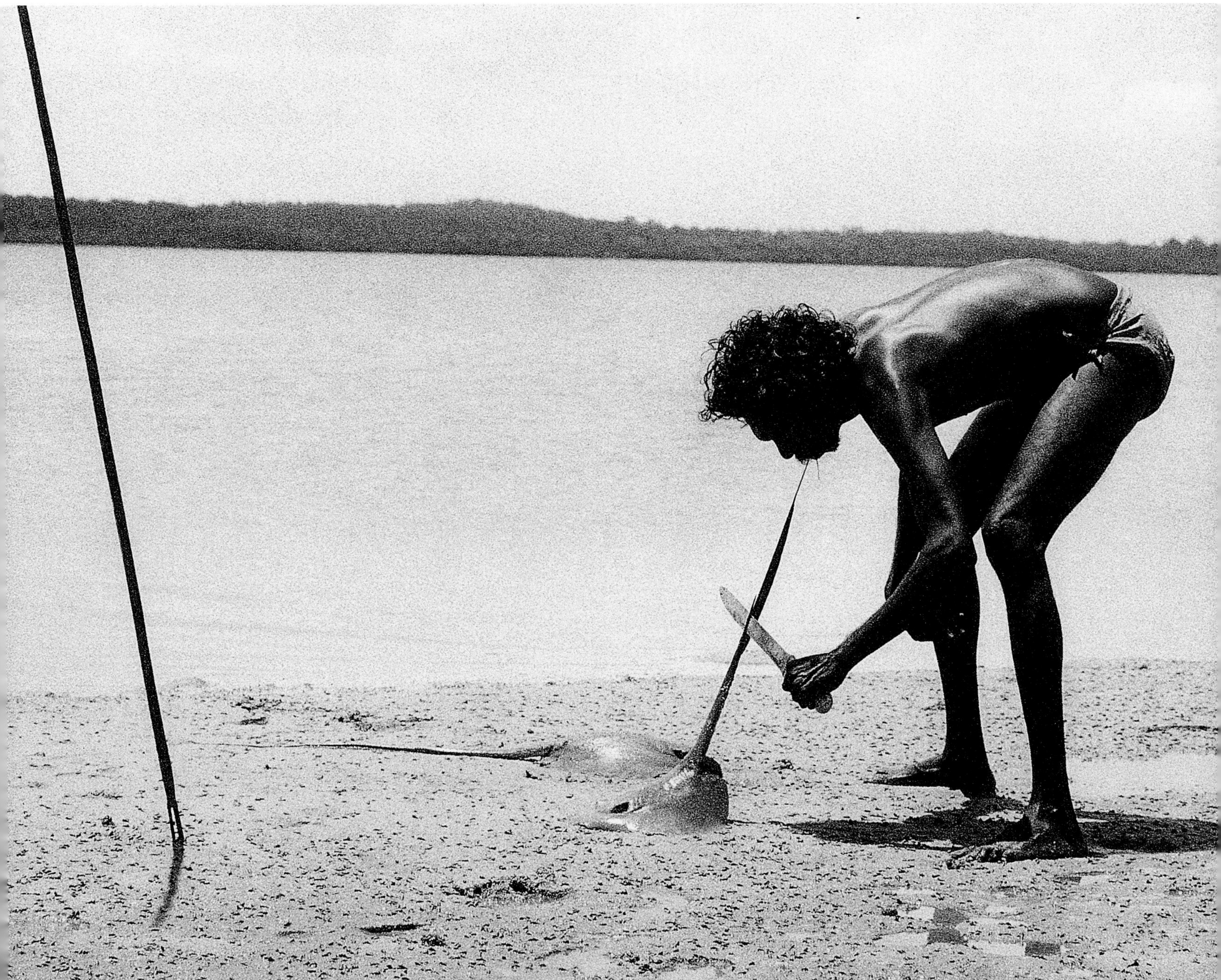

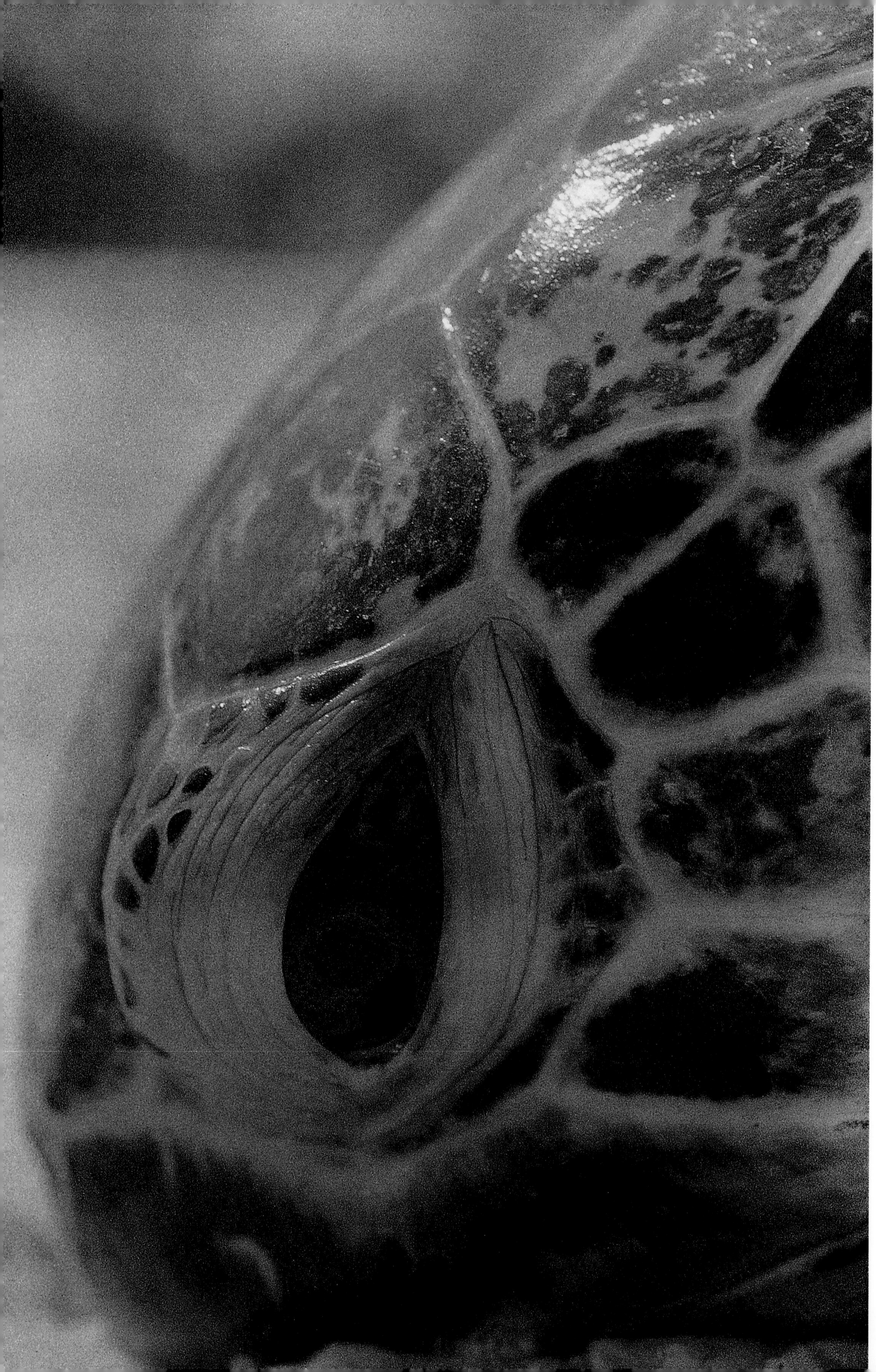

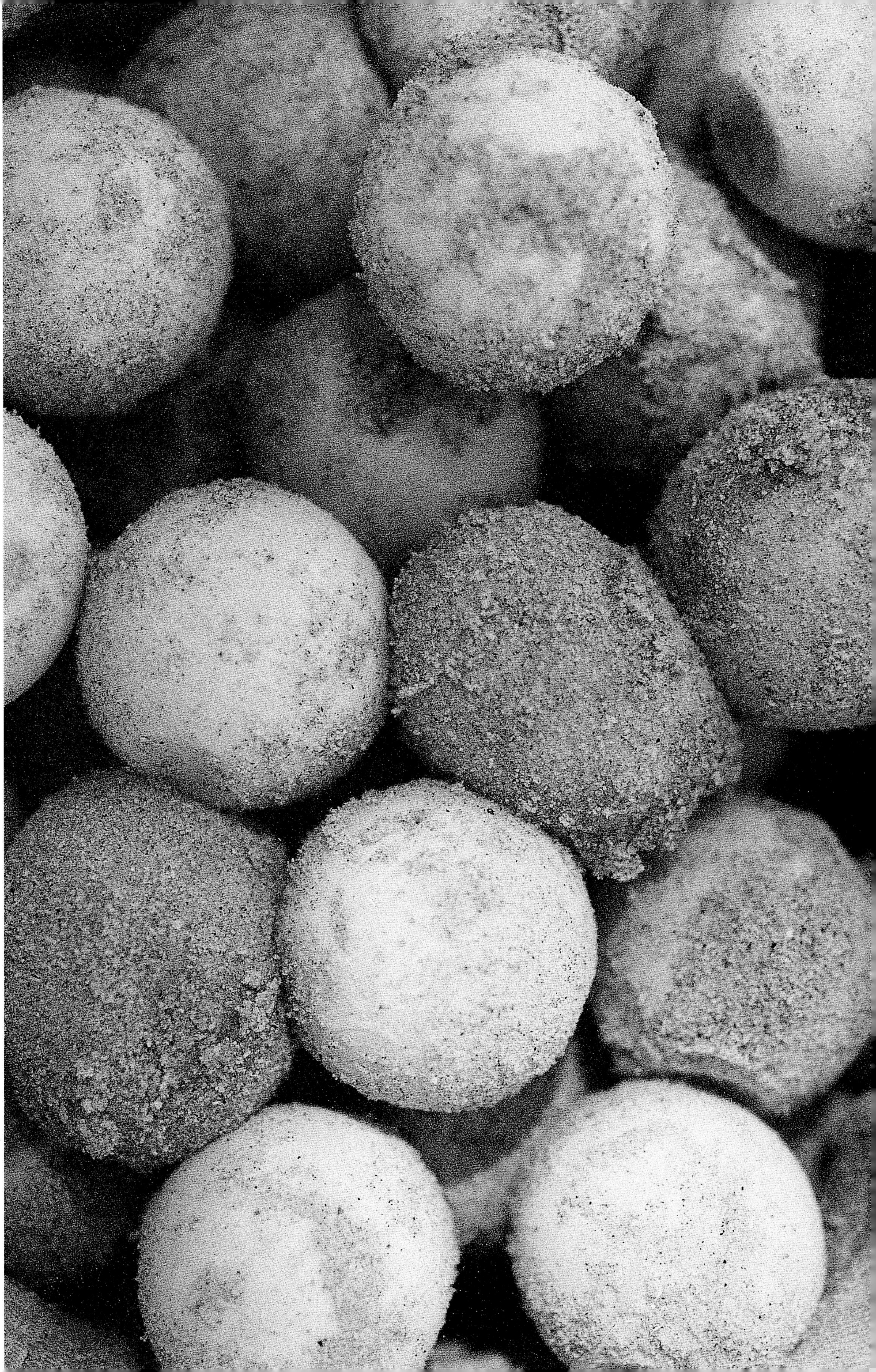

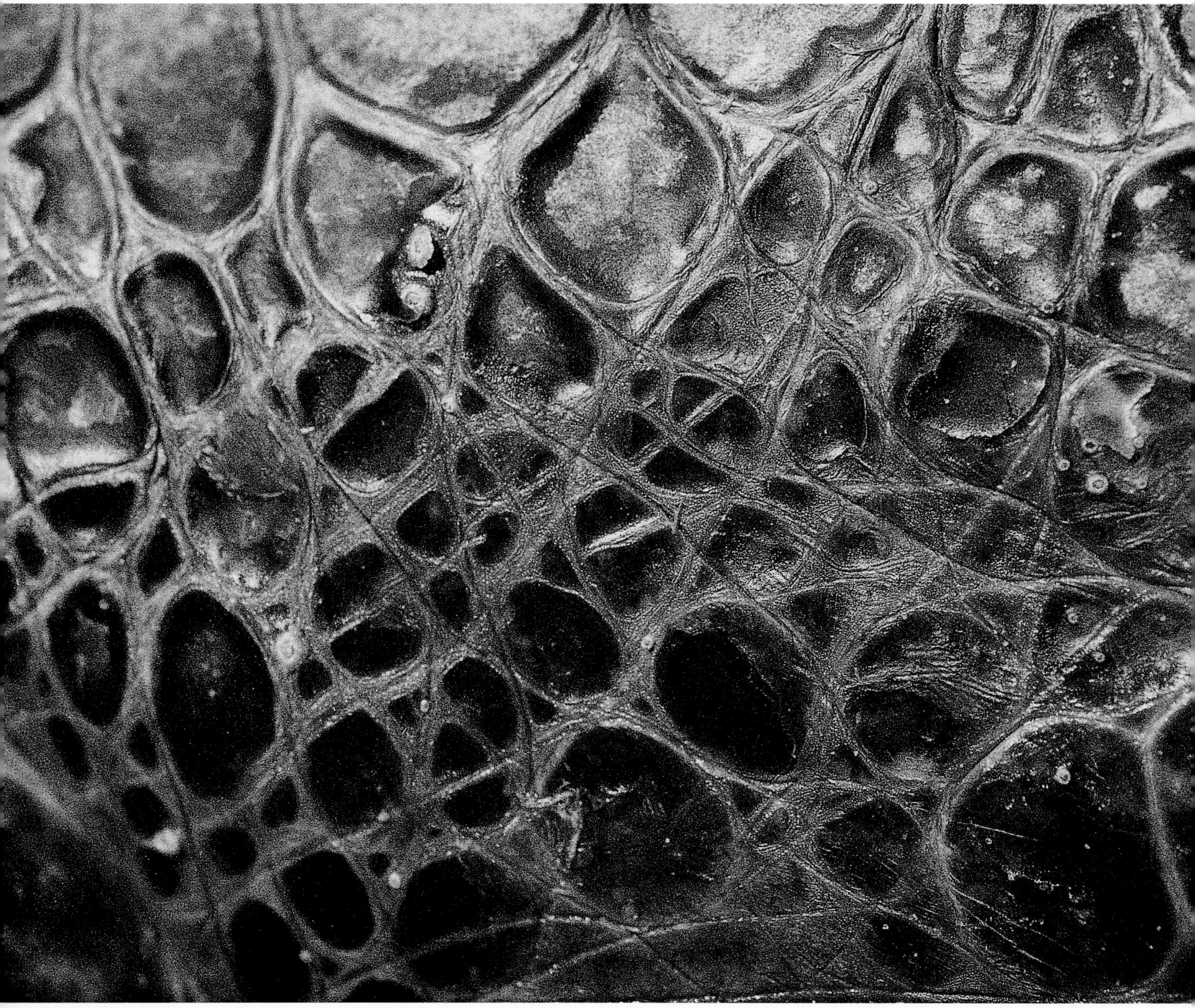

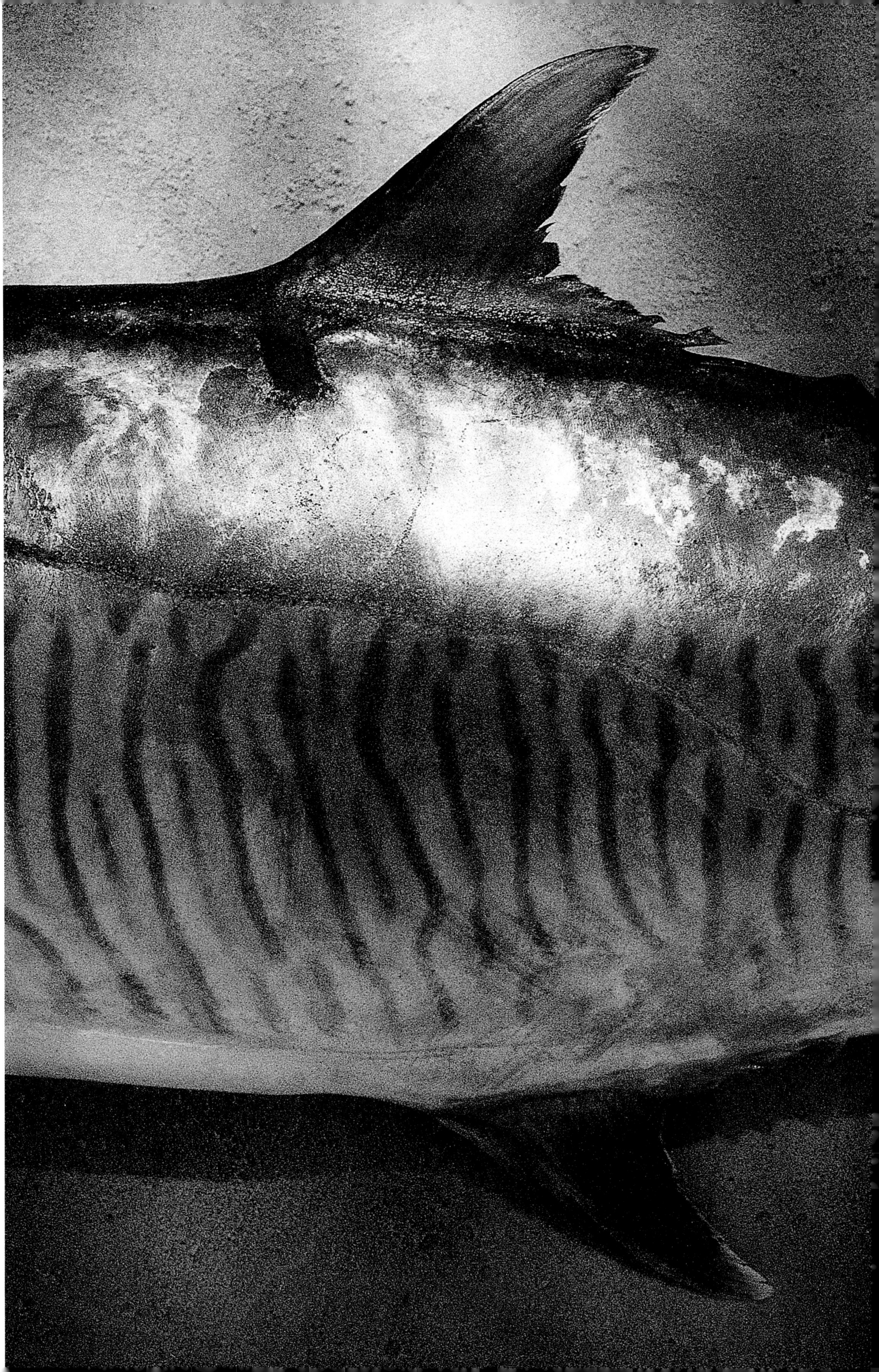

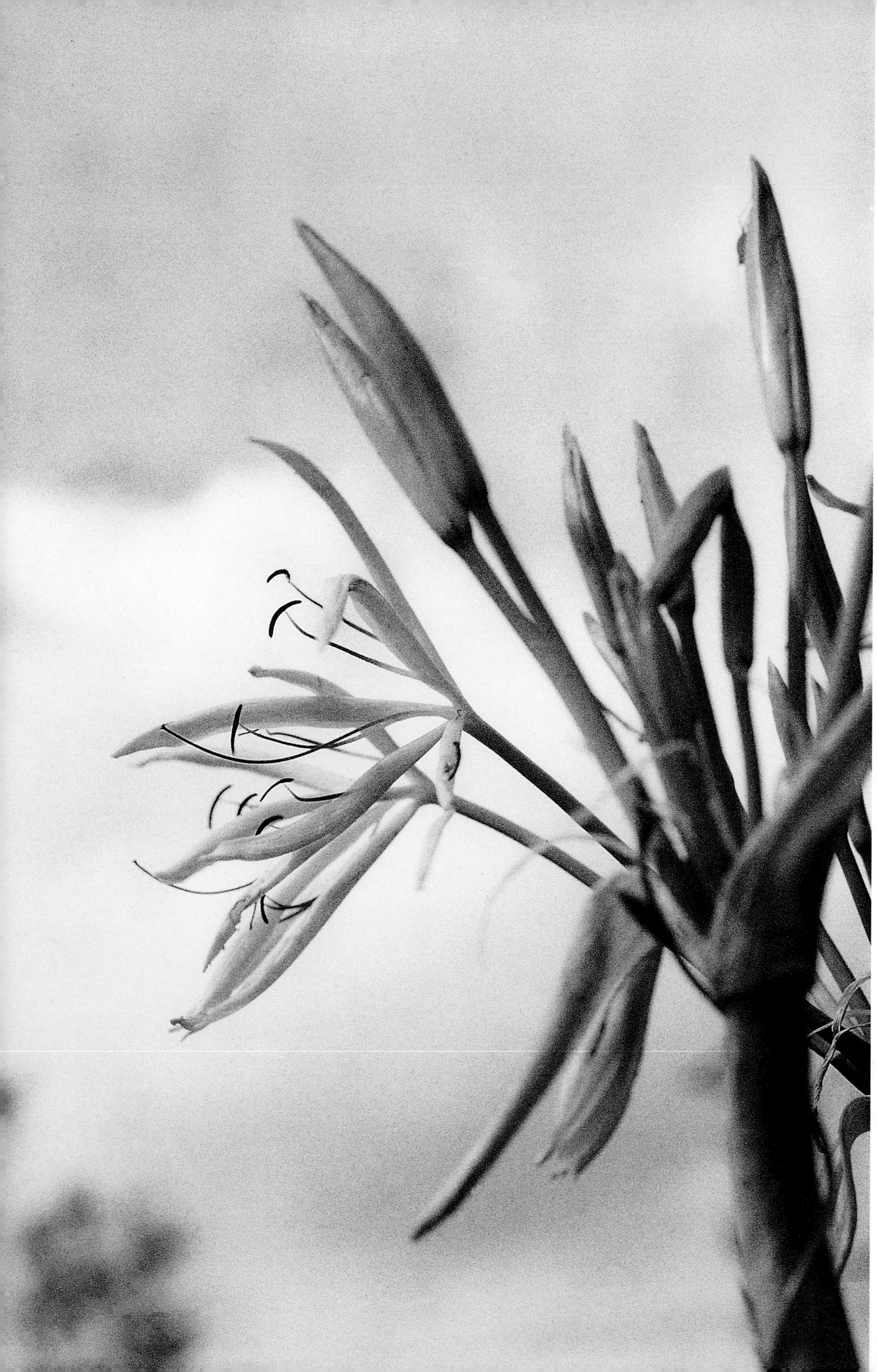

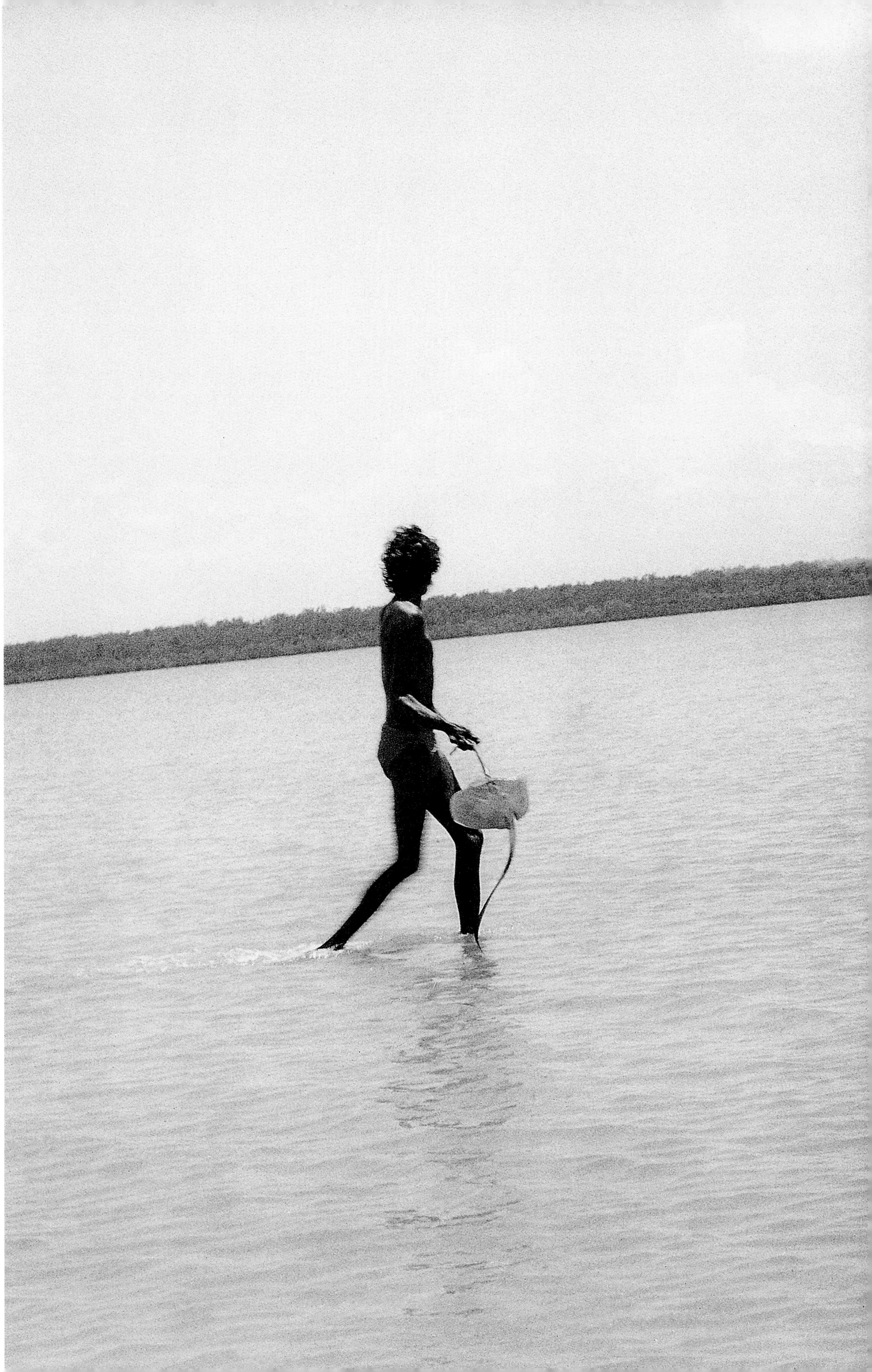

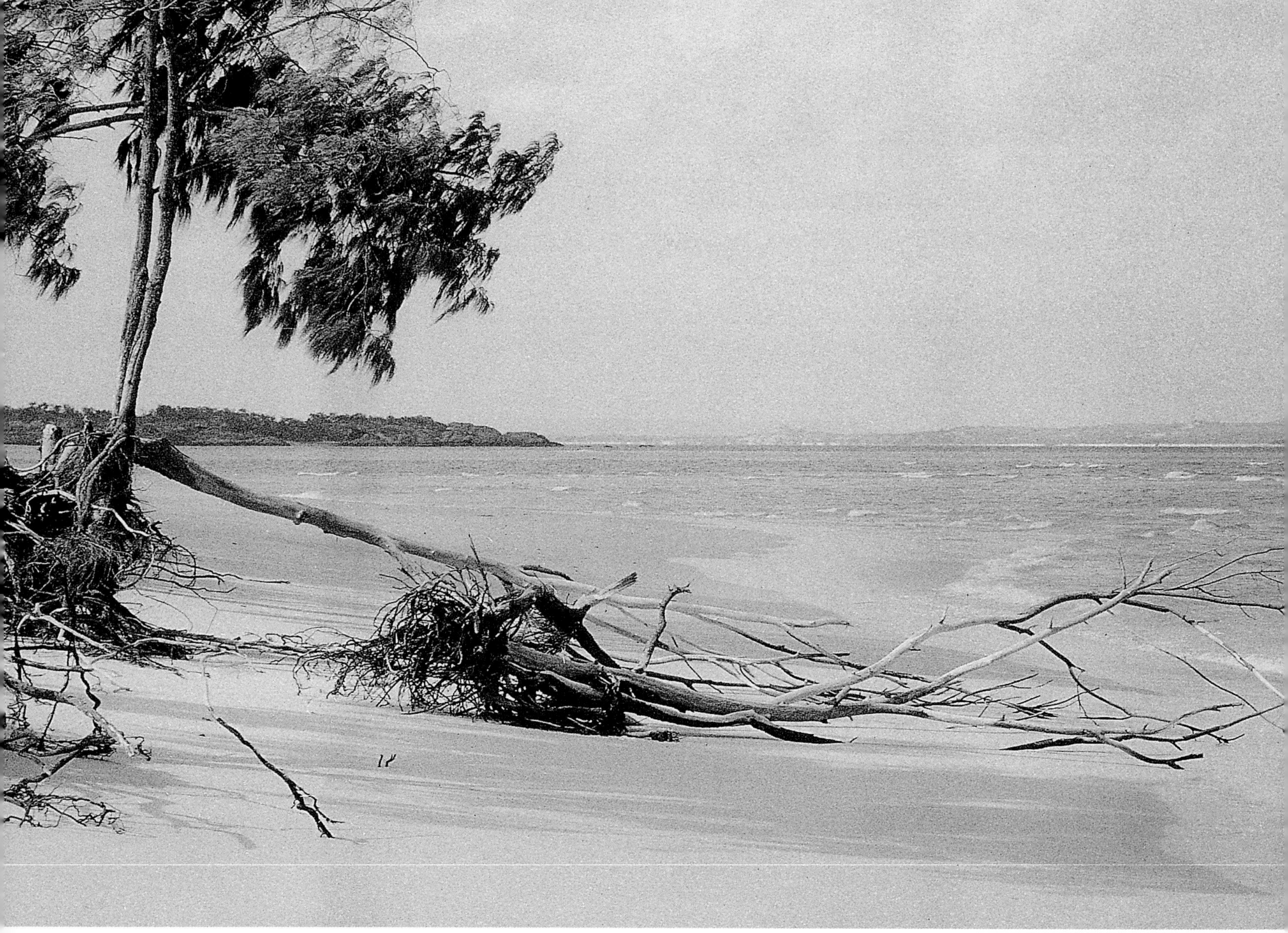

FLYING FOX

Flying fox is from this country, it's a totem. We dance for this one. Because there's so many of them you can catch them with a spear, or use woomera to club them, or a long stick. Climb up a tree by a mangrove with stick or woomera, take as many as possible and cook them under hot sand in underground oven with banana leaves.

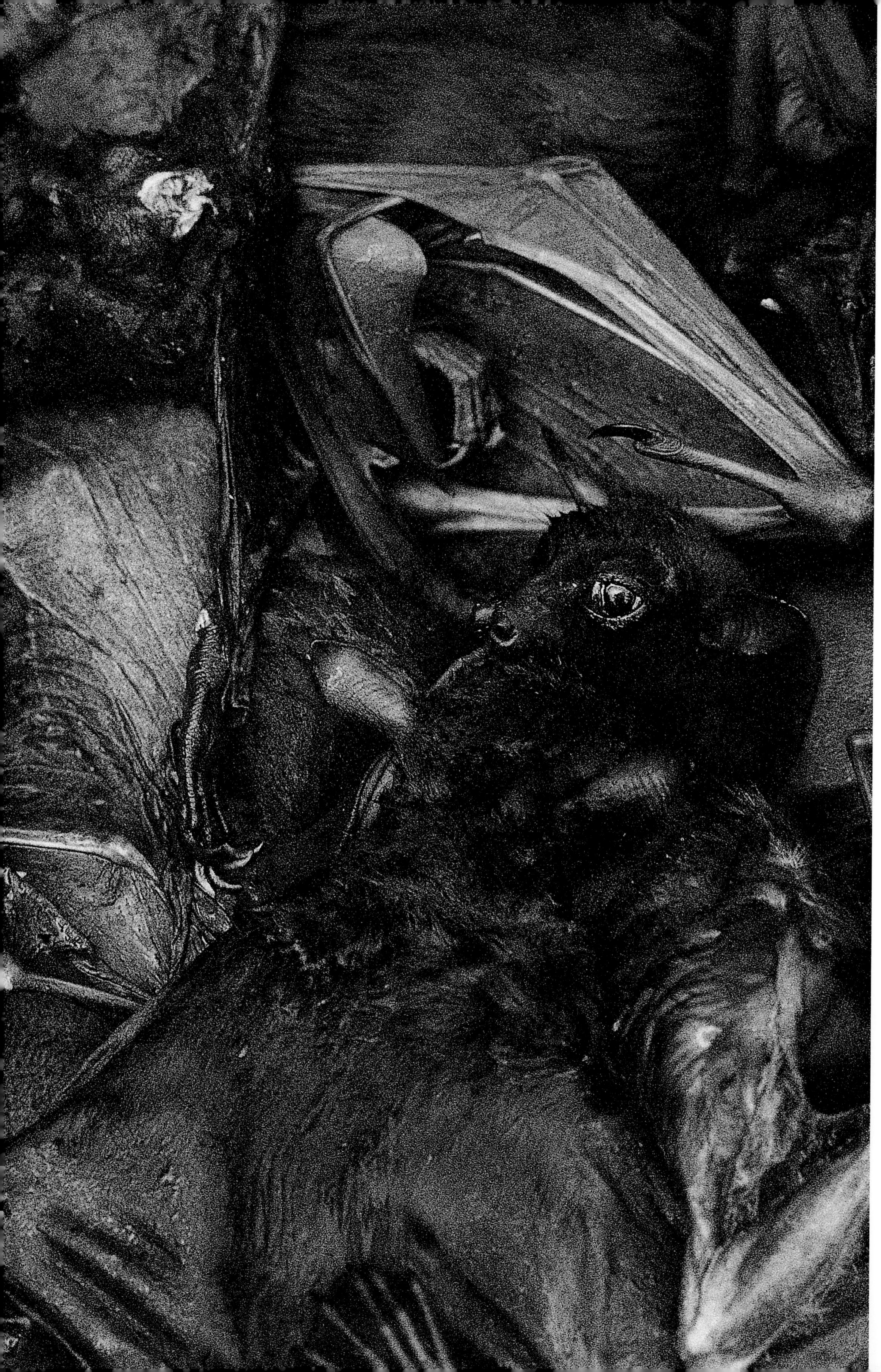

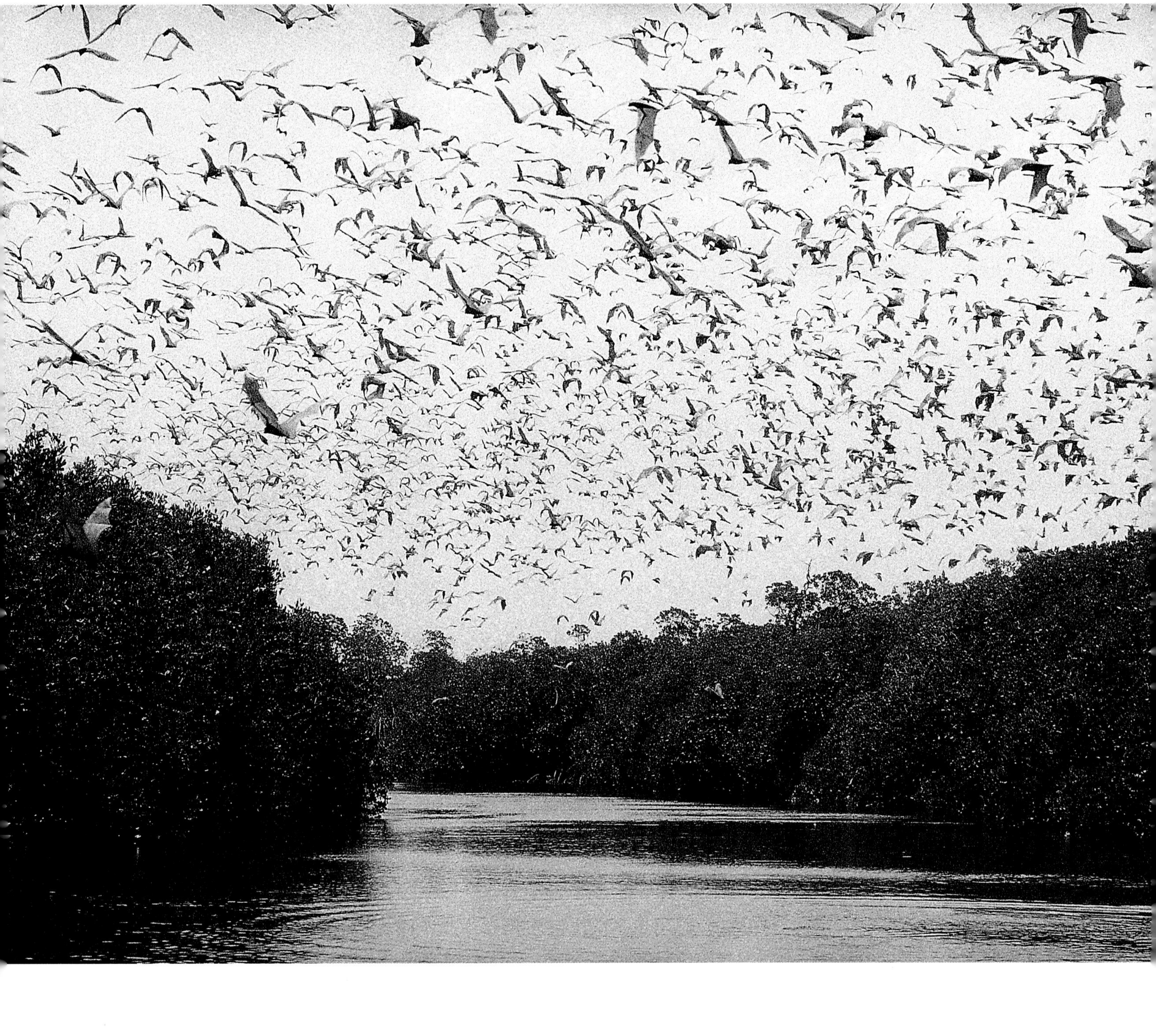

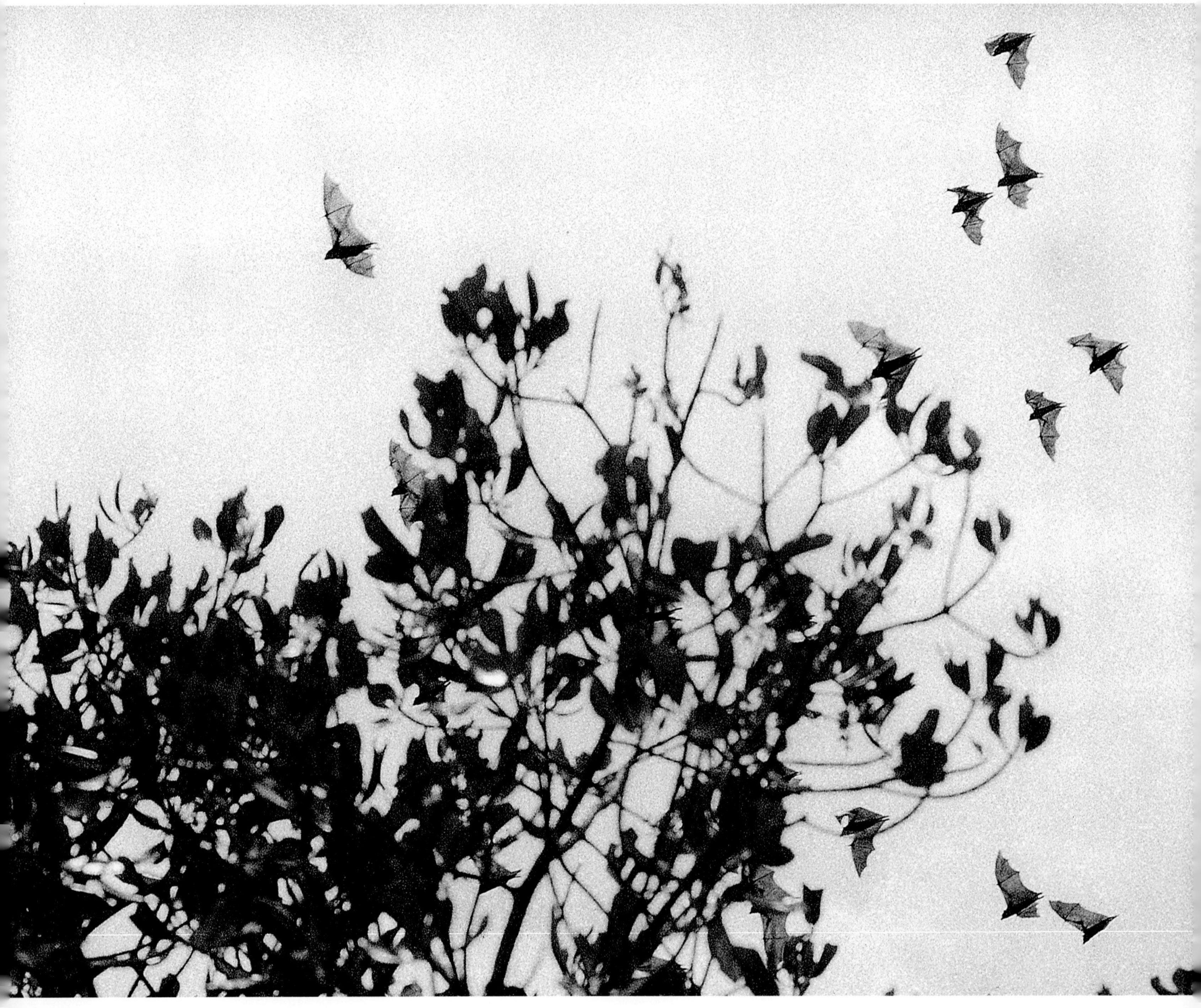

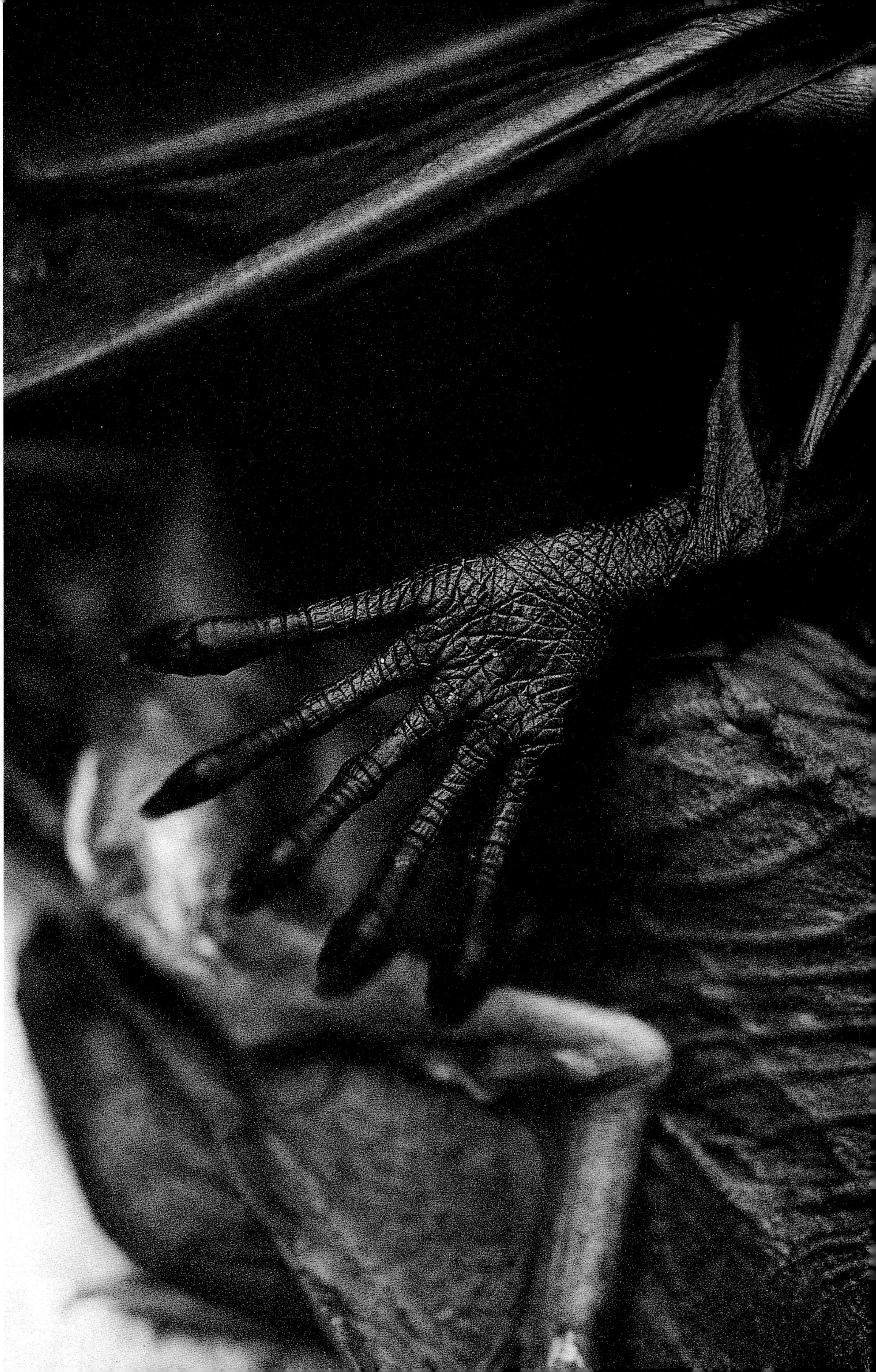

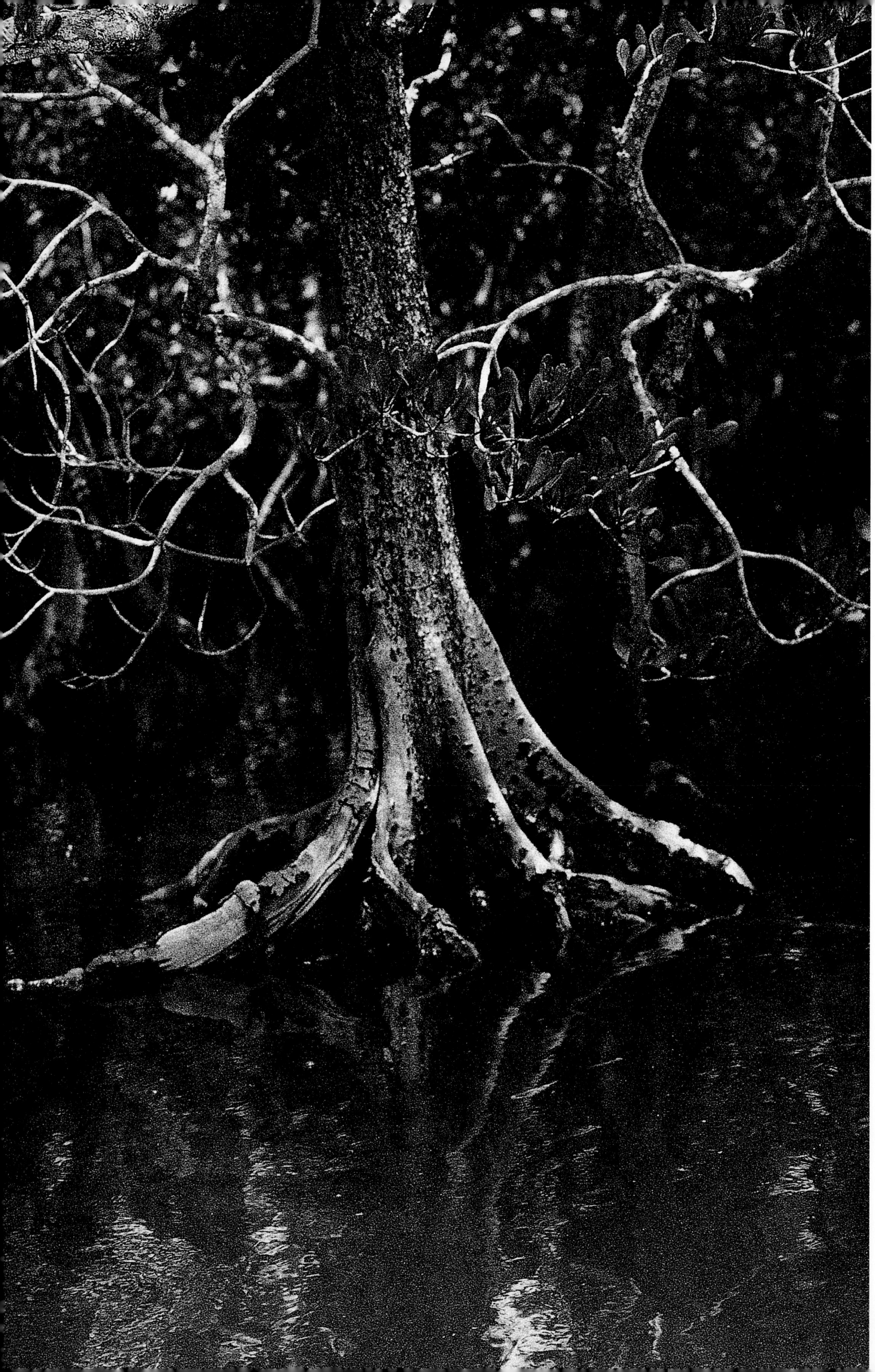

WILD HONEY

When it rains, witchetty grub comes out. We've got a belief that when you squash a Top End witchetty grub, a big rain comes. Not good for eating, this one, if it's hairy. If not hairy then it's okay to eat.

Small shark flower blossoms – back part is great medicine for sores, little cuts. Liquid in there is good for eyes; if you have sore eyes you rub it in. Just get a whole bunch of it raw, squeeze it and rub on.

When the stringybark flowers, you know it's wild honey time, that's a good time to go out. It comes when it's really hot, in the dry season. The honey is more creamy, frothy, like a cappuccino. Eat too much honey, it will make you real thirsty. Got to take a lot of water with you when you go out hunting for it. You have to have good eyes to follow the bee. In the morning and evening the bee doesn't come out, best day to go out is when it's really hot because they buzz around. They don't sting, these ones.

Sea eagle, we don't hunt that one. Not as big a totem as shark or crocodile, but sea eagles have more stories in them. Traditionally they have always been friends.

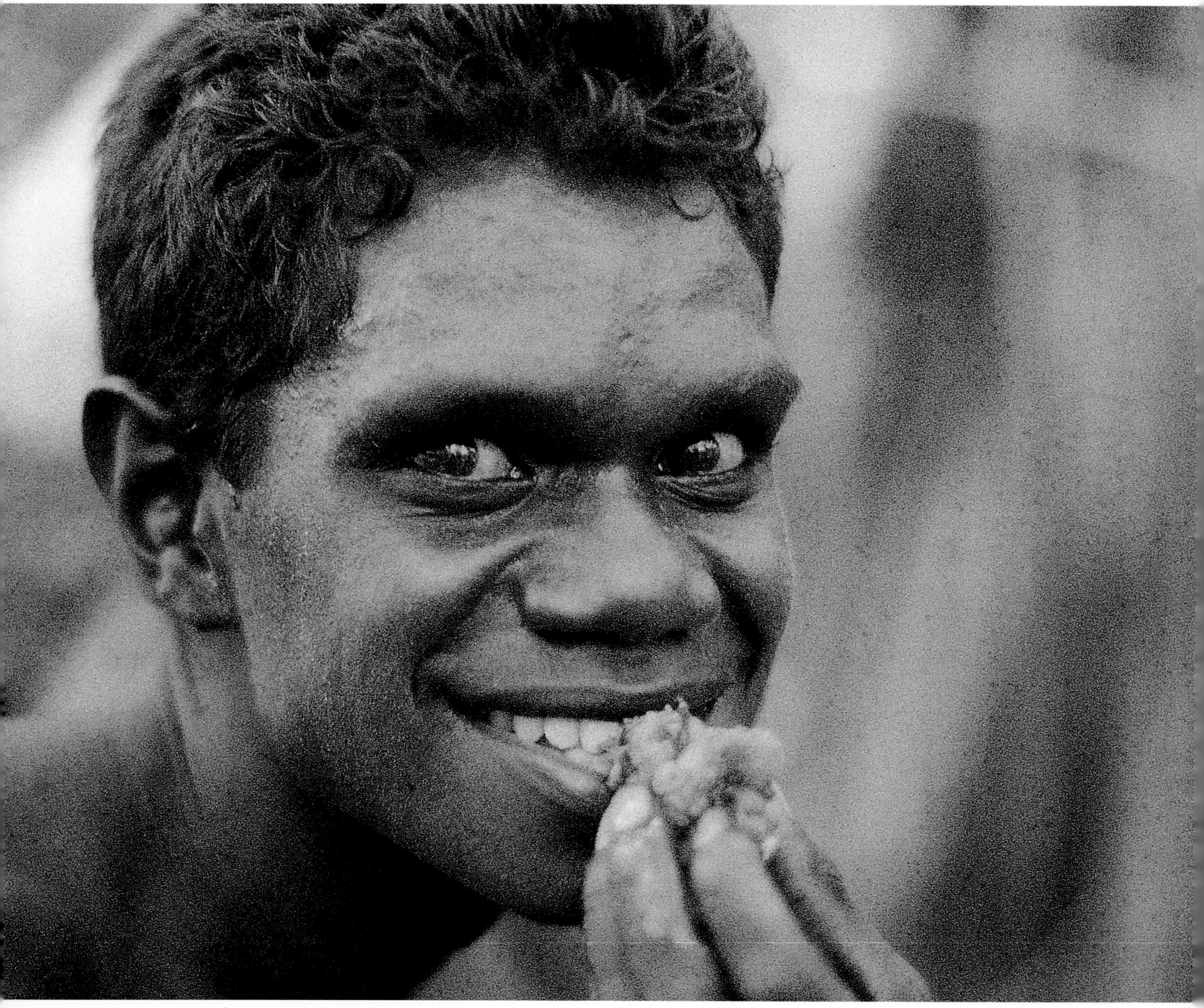

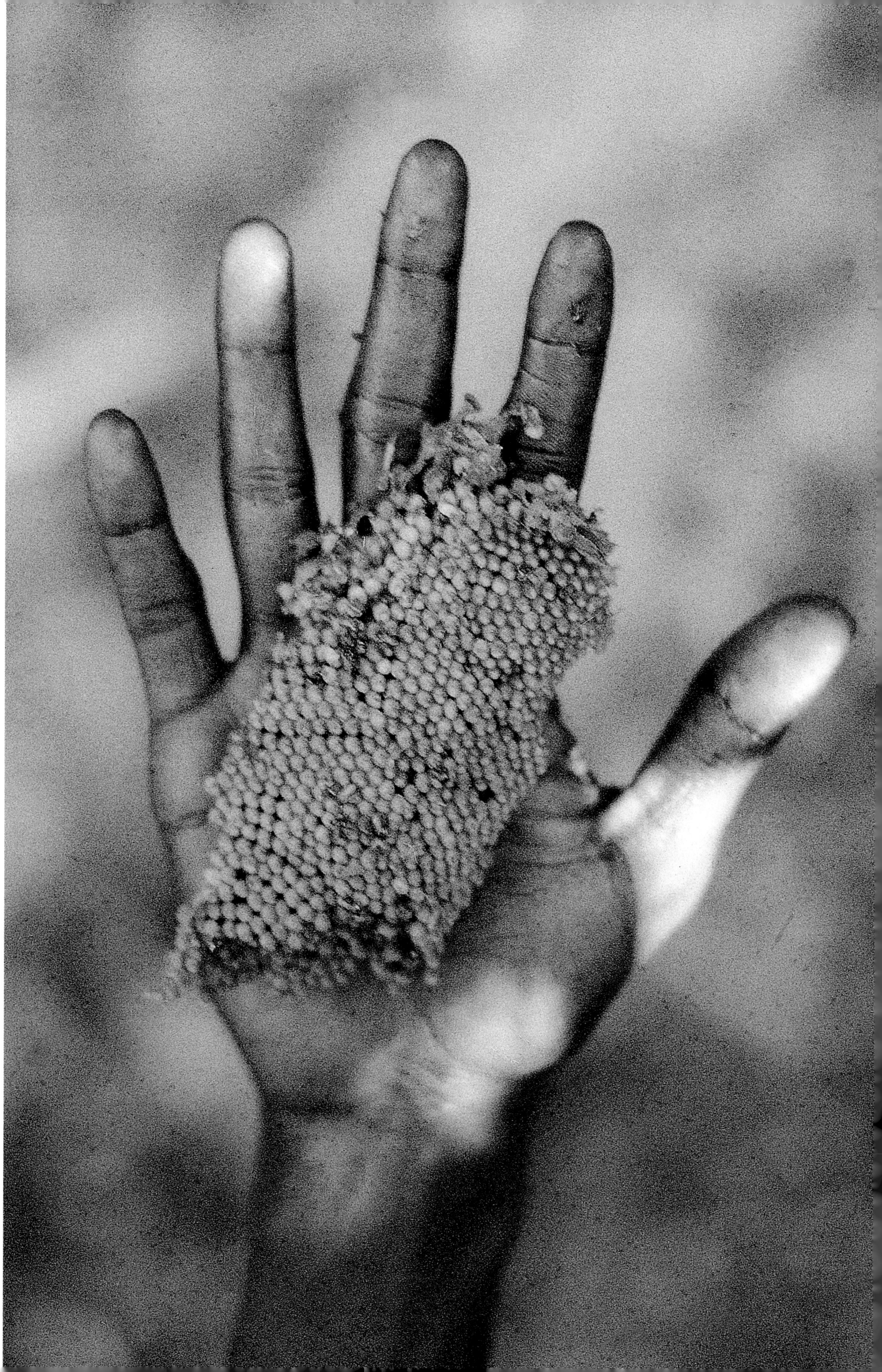

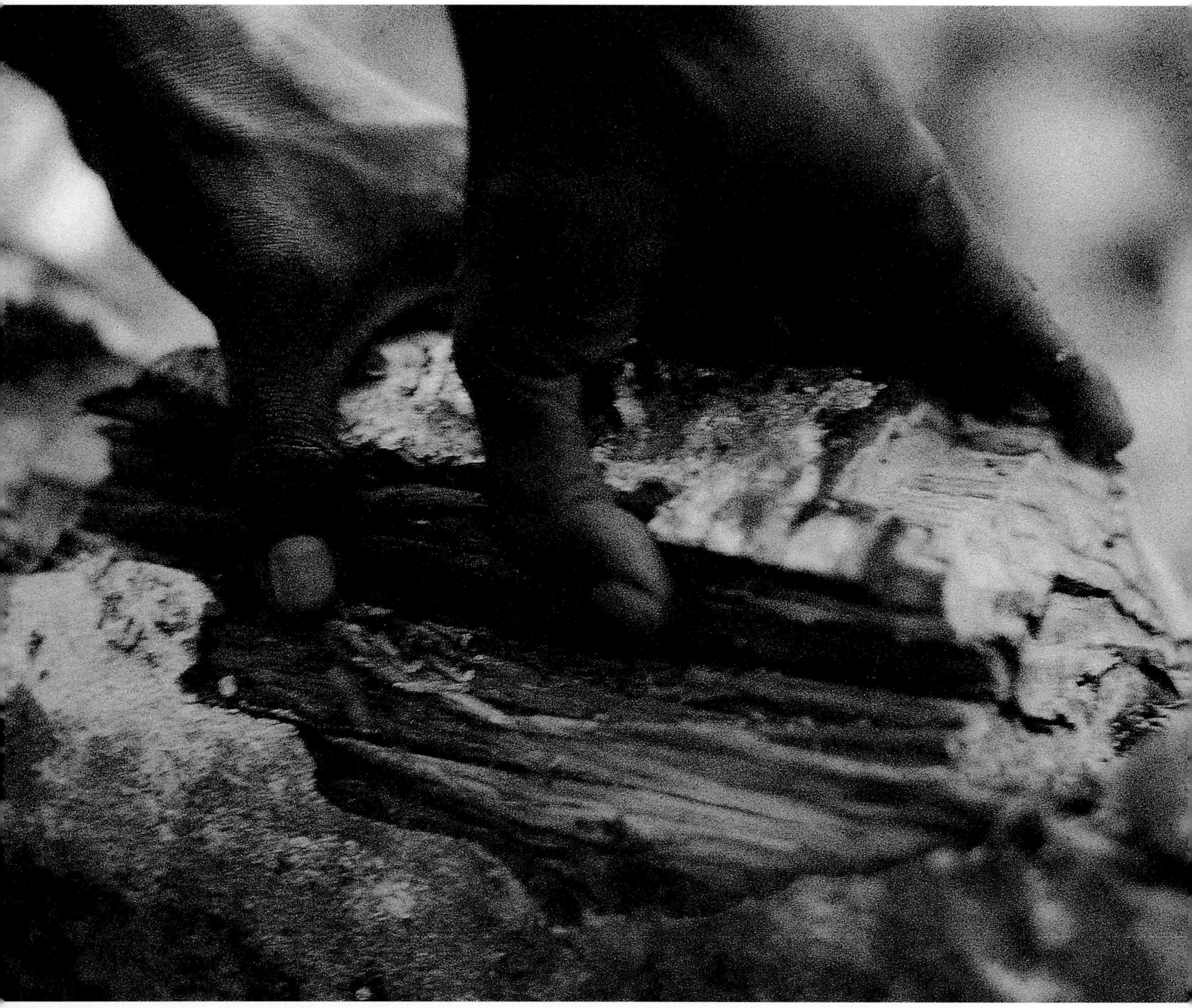

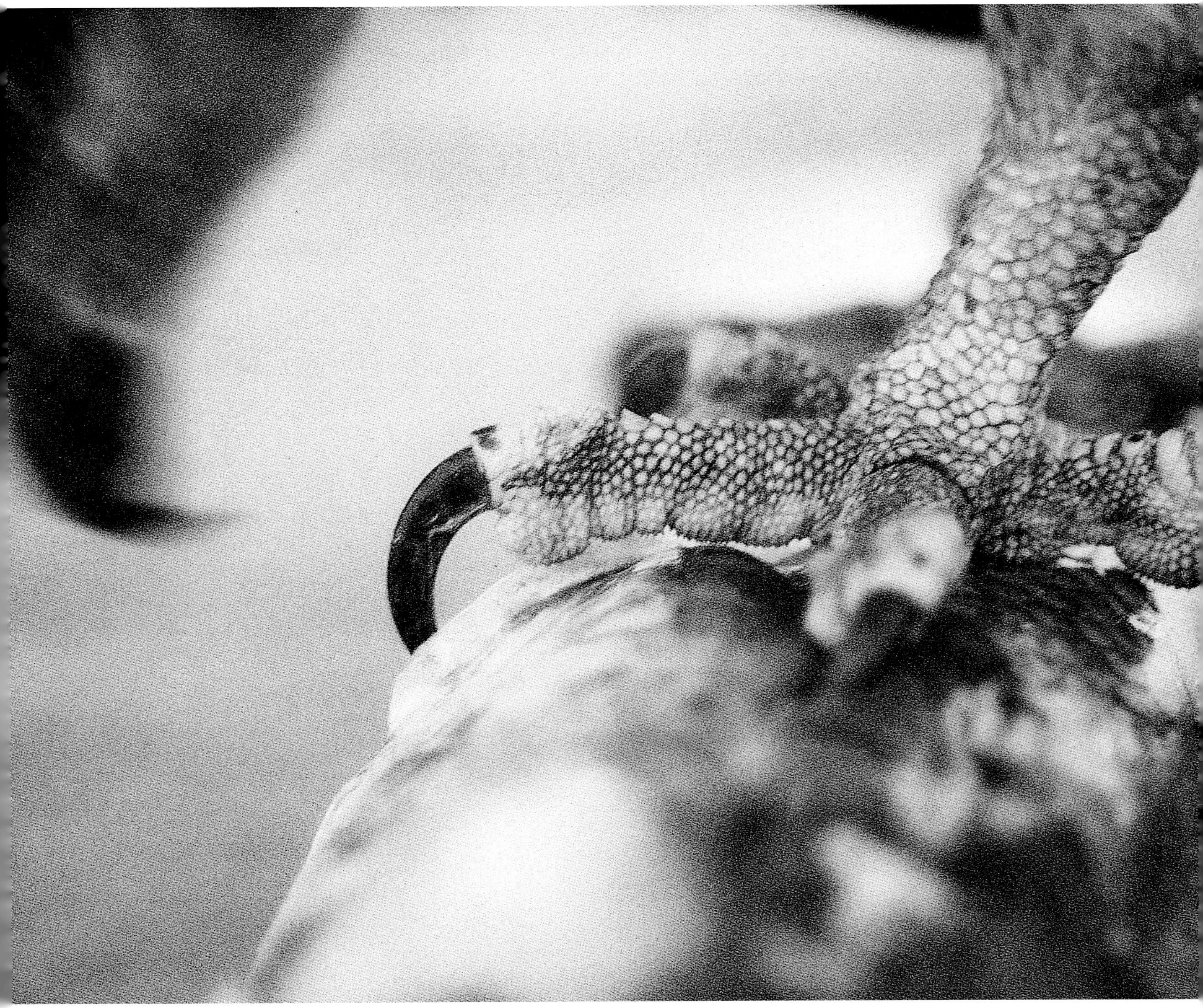

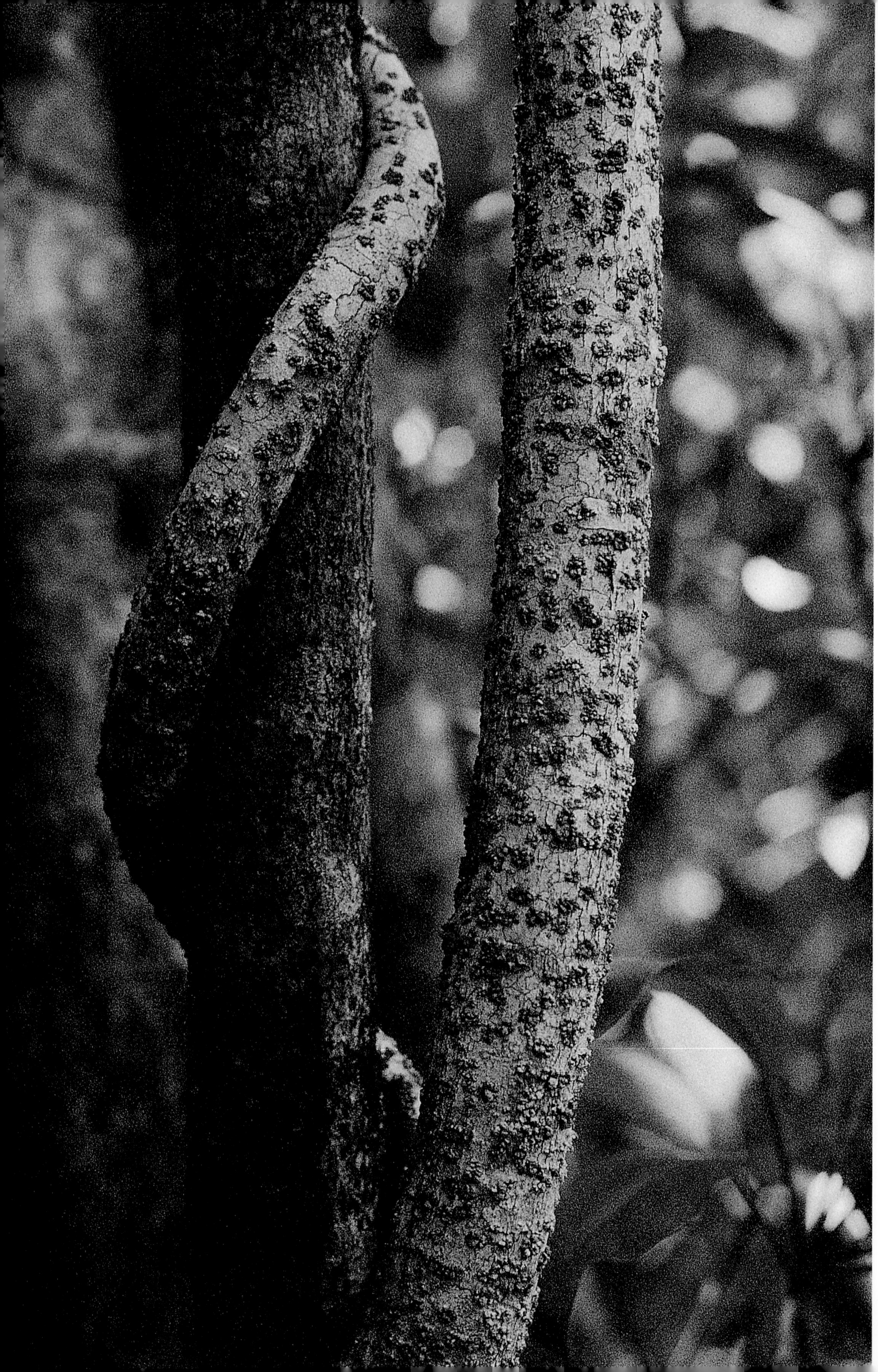

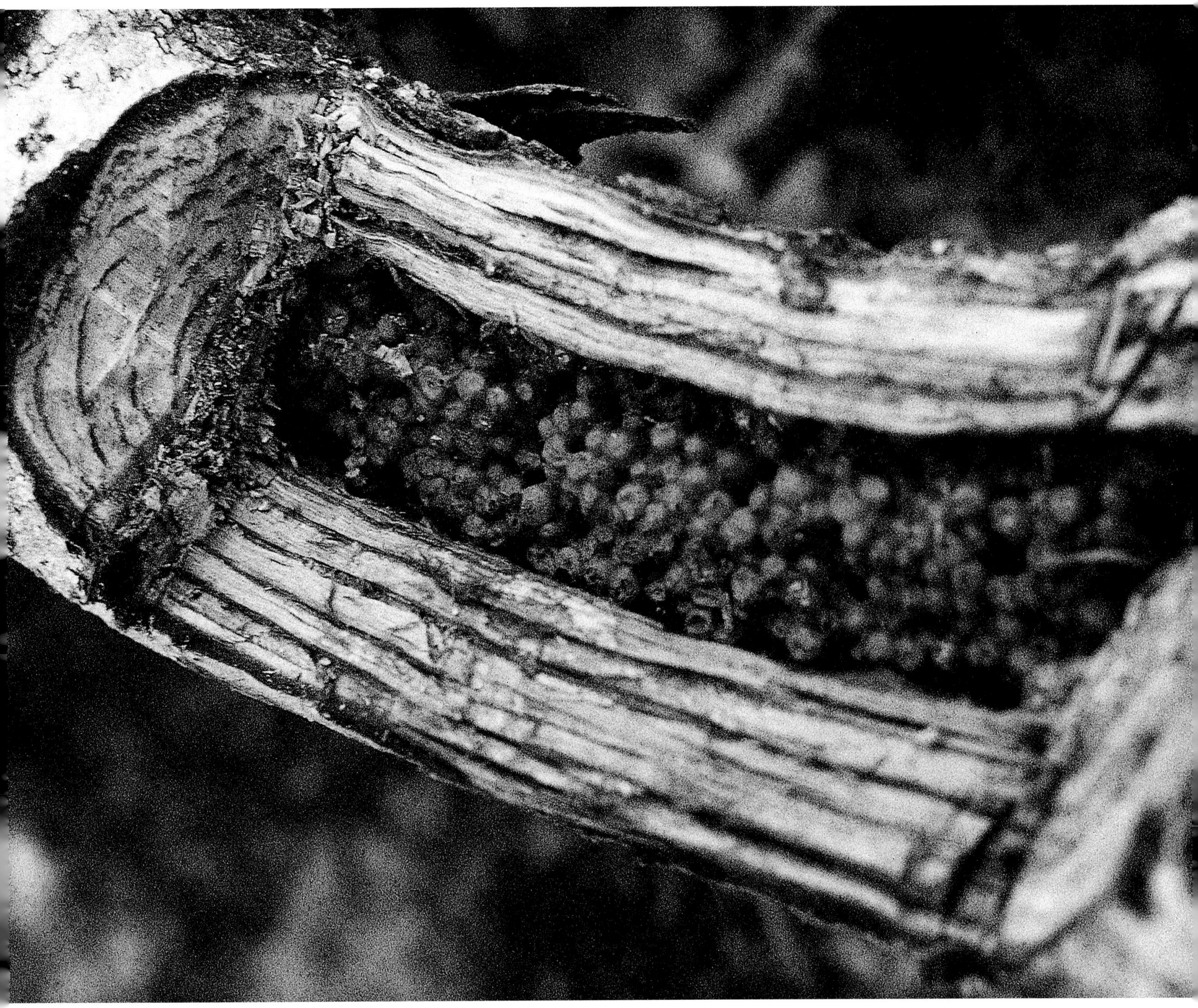

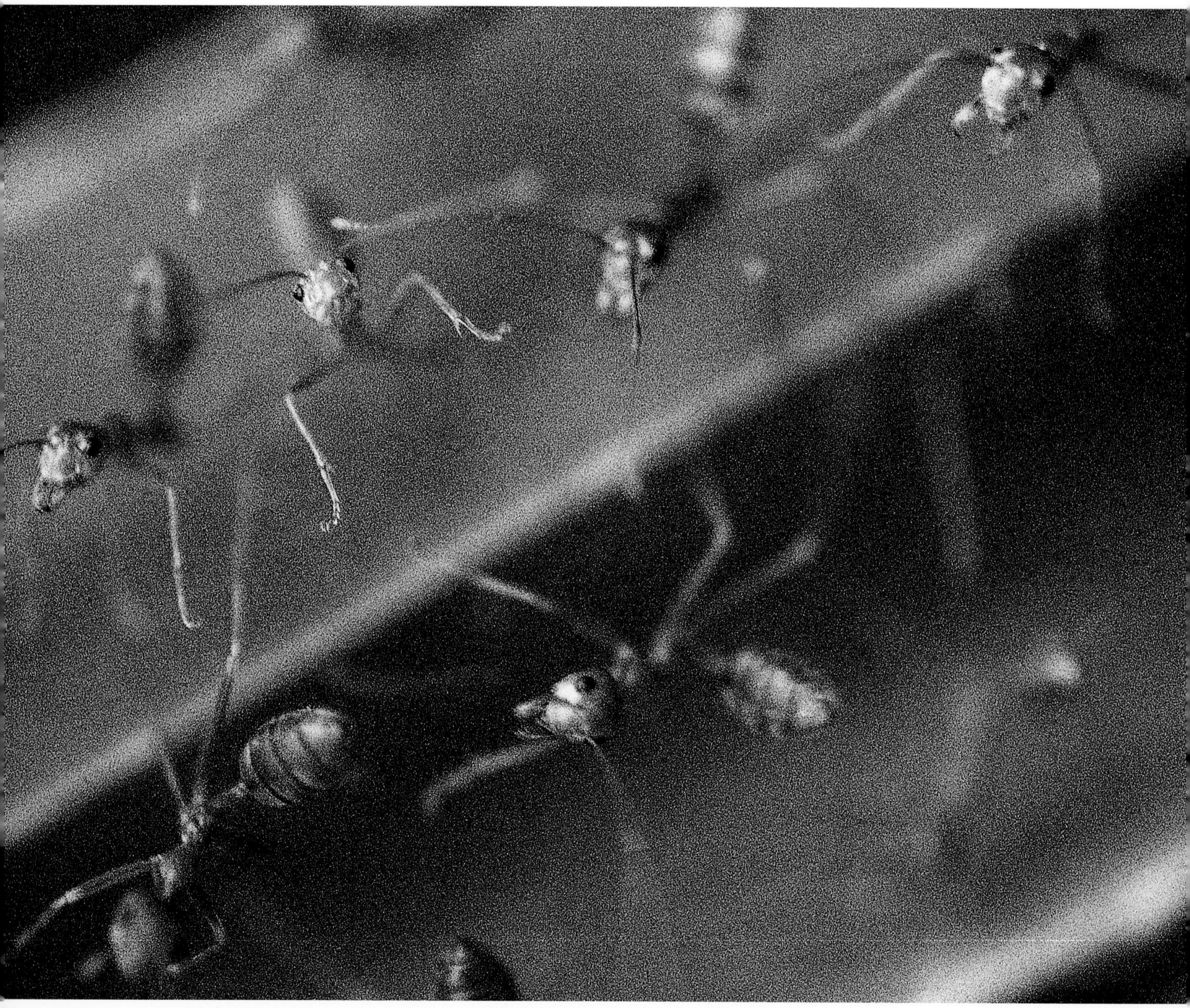

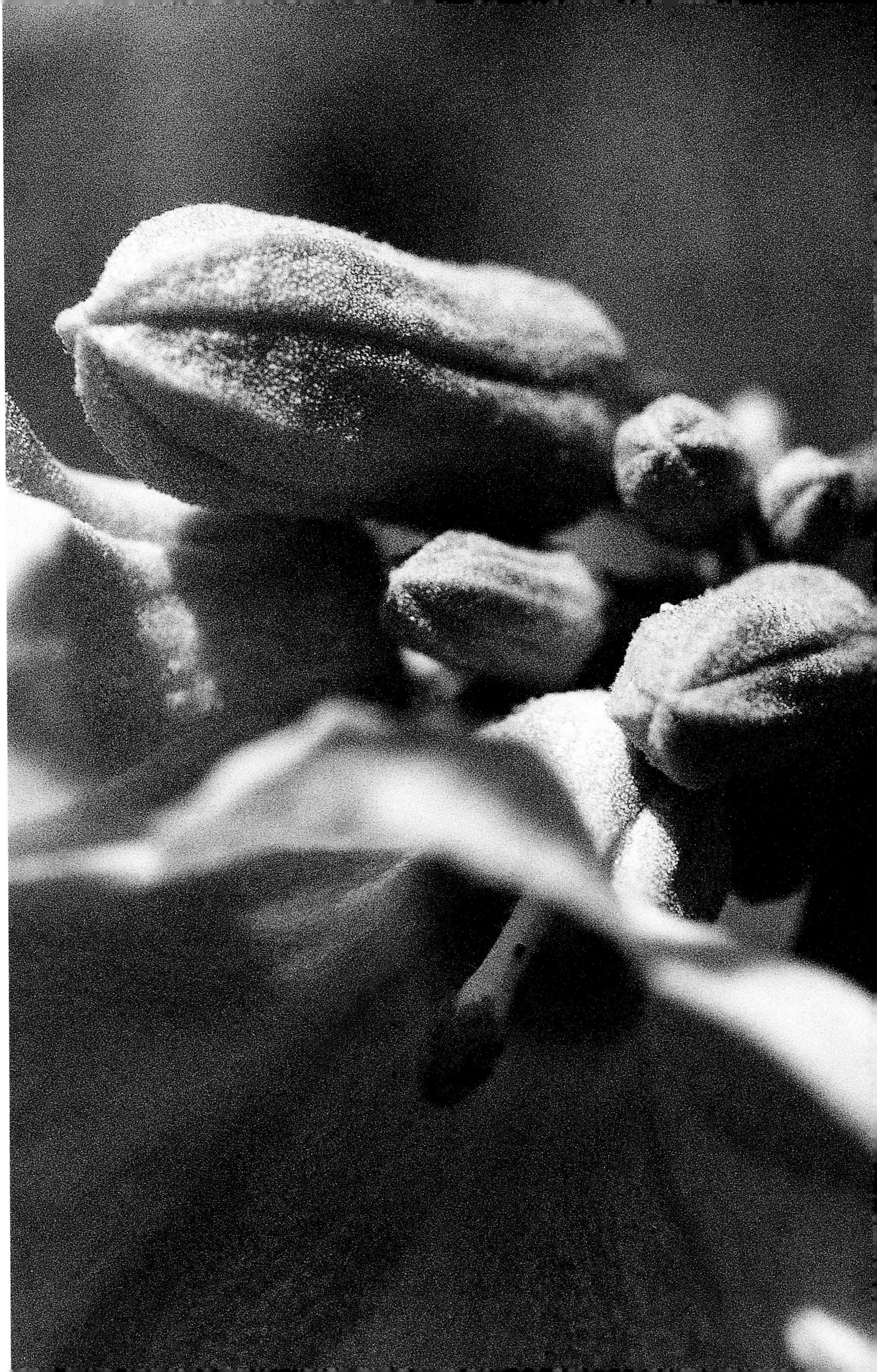

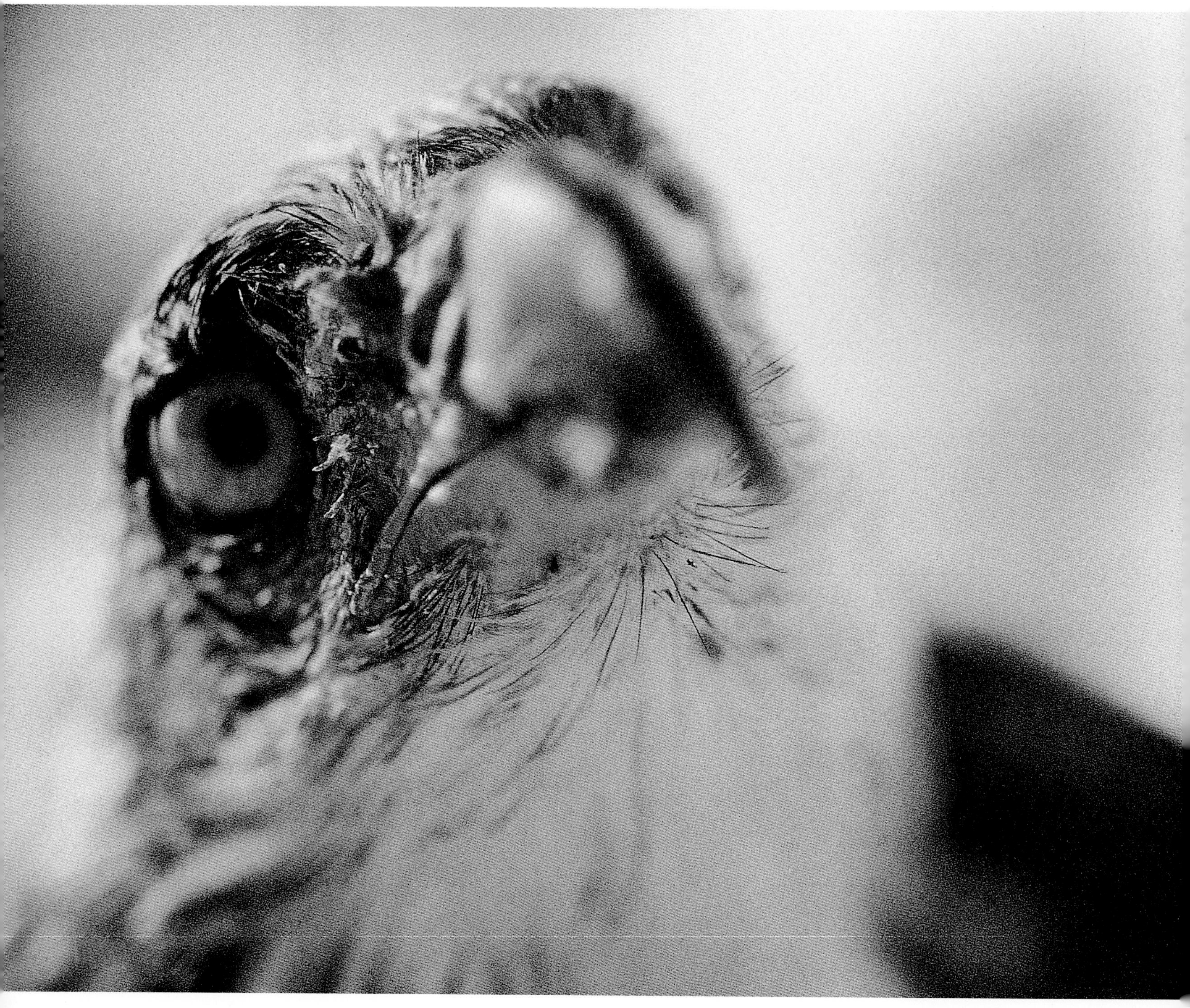

KANGAROO HUNTER

Men paint their bodies to disguise their smell – the animals smell only the paint. Hunt with shovel-nose spear and woomera. Don't hunt with boomerang, only in the centre of Australia do they use it. Sometimes kangaroo is dangerous because of feet; they use their legs to kick. Red one is more dangerous, red kangaroo is a totem in Arnhem Land.

Cook kangaroo on top of fire first, on rocks, to burn off hair. Then cut it open, take the guts out, and cook flat – put heated rocks inside ribcage. Organs are eaten, liver, heart, kidney. Leg bones of calf are sharpened and used by women when someone dies, for mourning. Blood of kangaroo is put on dog to make it like a hunter. When kangaroo is wounded, the dog can chase.

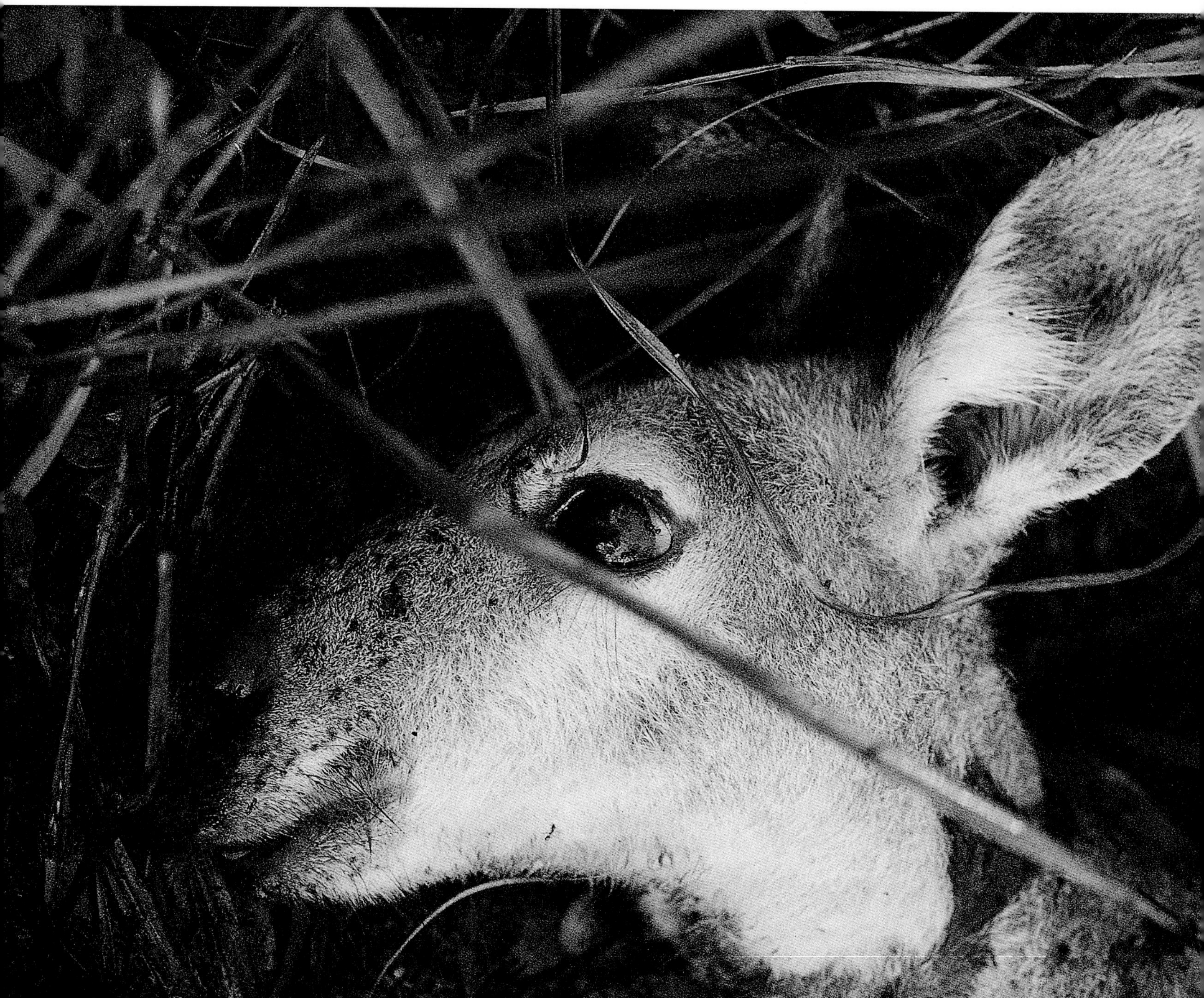

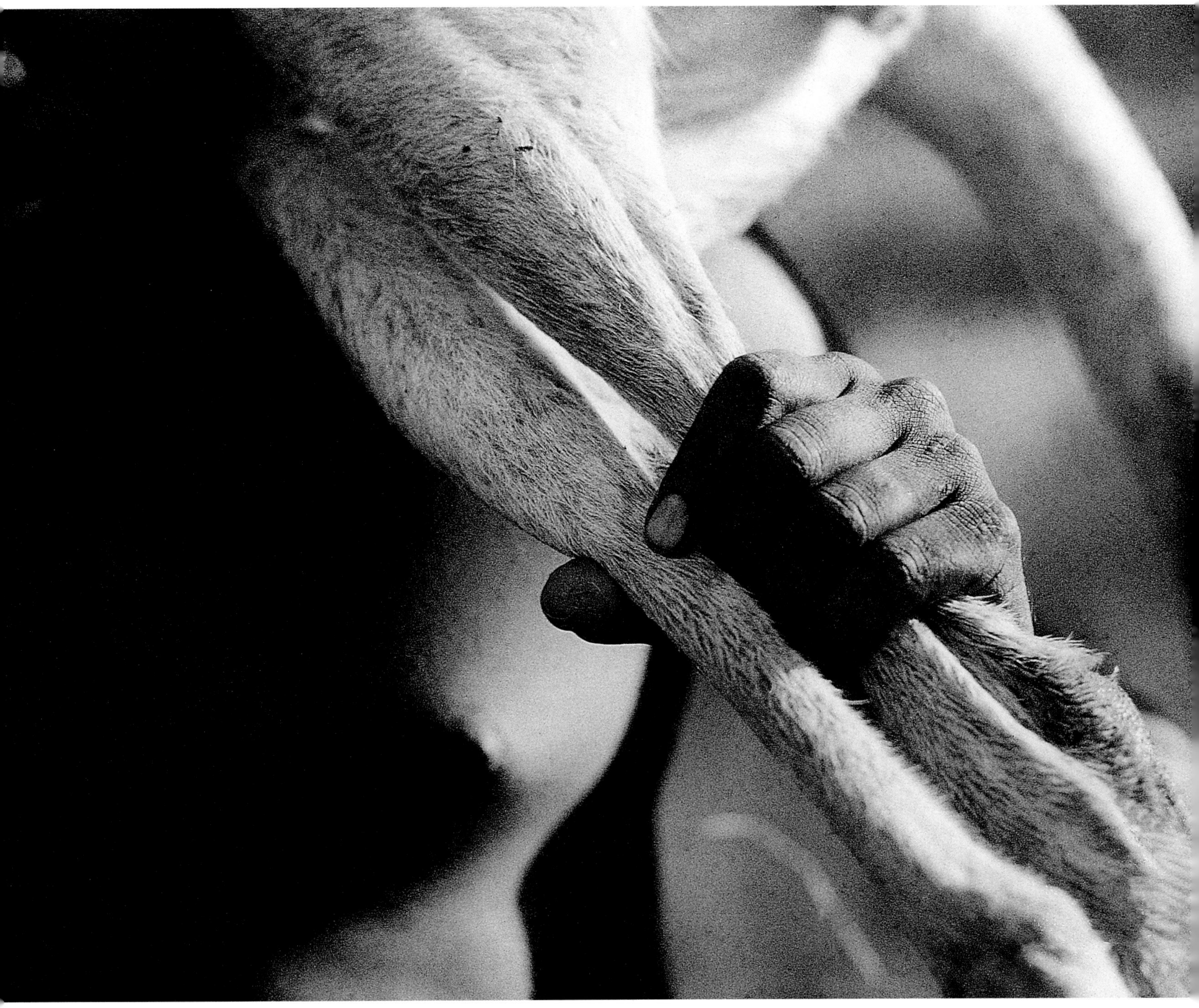

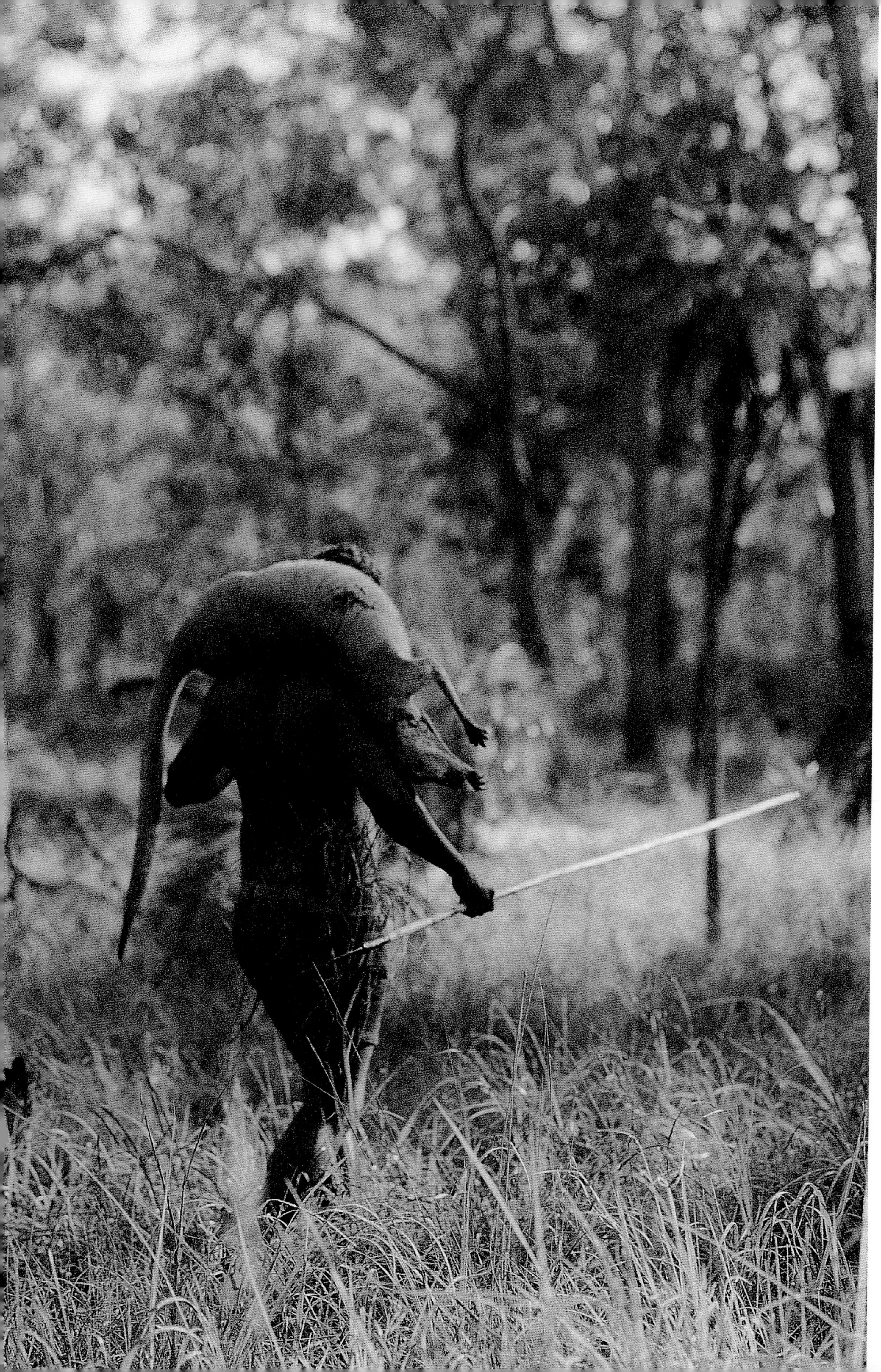

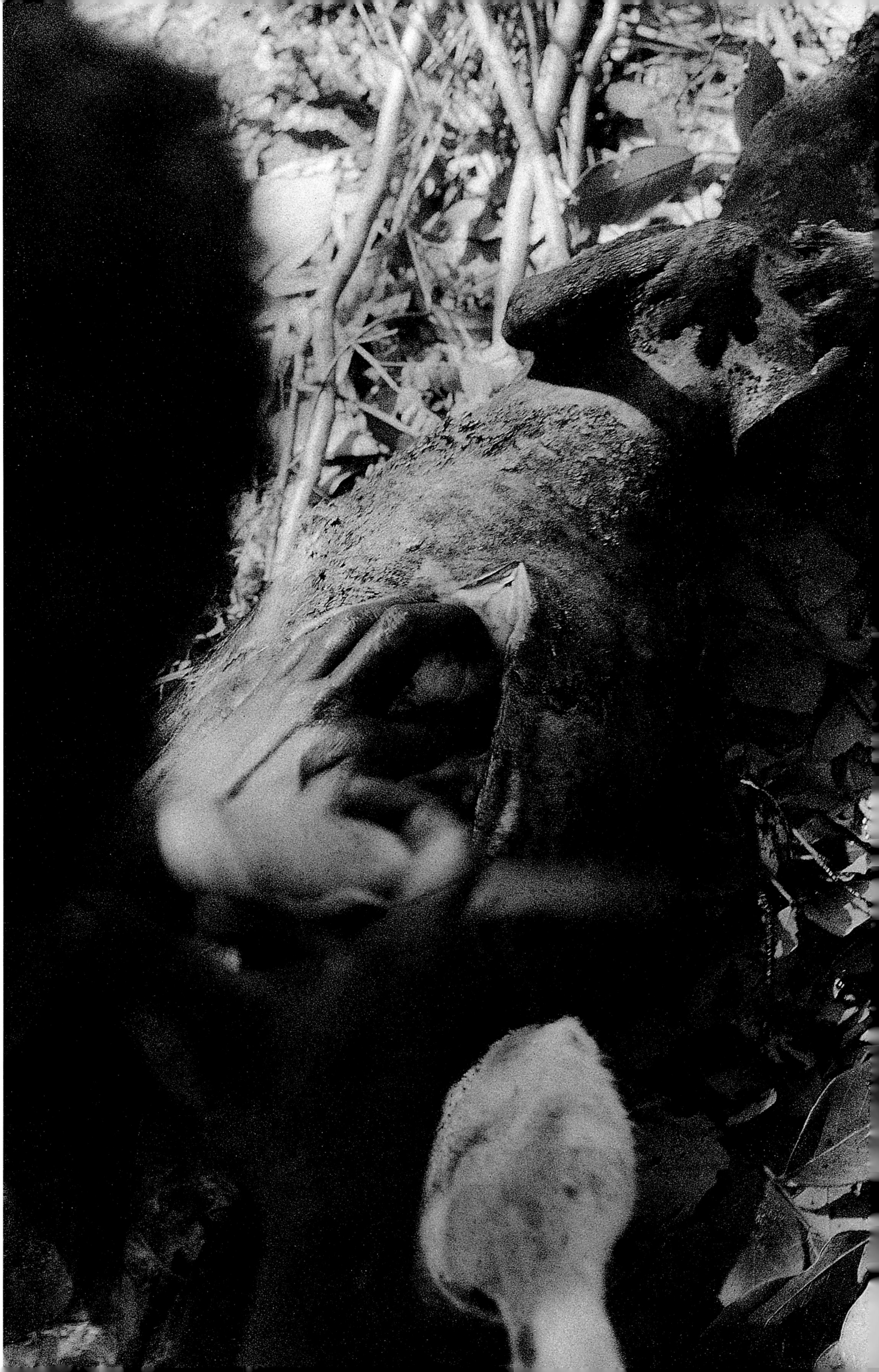

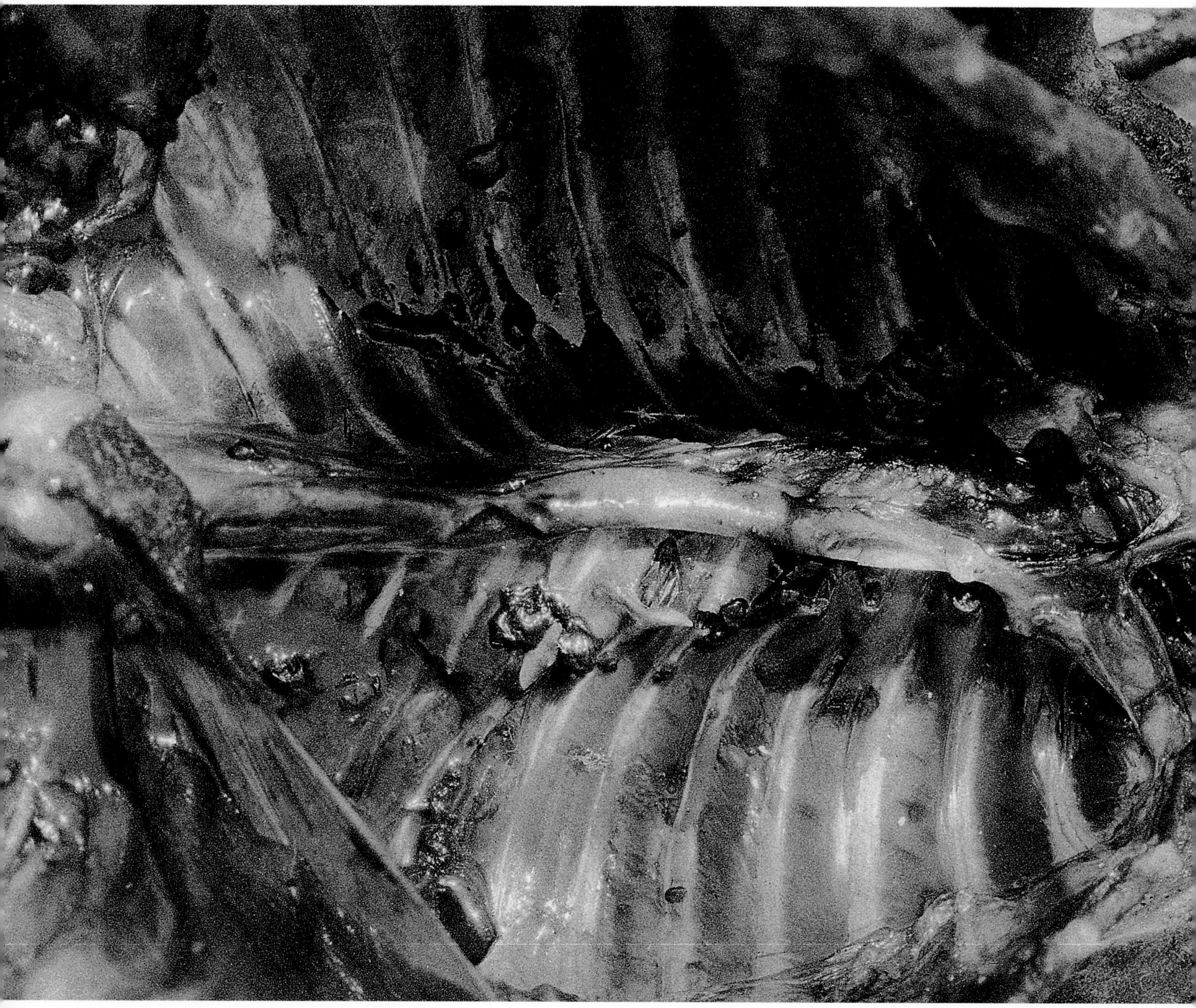

AFTER BUSHFIRE

Cycad is very old, one of the main food sources. A lot of stories and songs for this one found in Top End and north-west. Tropical green mostly, no problem with fire. It just keeps coming back, it all dies down and just grows back. Make bread from the seed, takes a few days to prepare. Mainly old people do this because it makes you sick, very ill, if you don't prepare it properly. Have to soak it in still water. The bread is very special.

Stringybark is the main tree for honey. Honey comes from a lot of other little trees but stringybark contains more. The bark is used for bark painting, or when crushed in special cleansing ceremony. Burn the bark to make it straight for painting. For cleansing, make a fire with rocks on it and burn the wet bark and sit around the fire, put a cover over it and breathe the steam. You can do this after a circumcision, part of a cleansing ritual, or if you're stressed or depressed, or if kids are doing bad things. Similar to Native American people's sweatlodge. You can bite the stringy part of the bark while it is on the fire, cleans your mouth. Bigger stringybark trees you can make a canoe out of, or build sheds or houses. The tree dies after you take bark, but it doesn't die for no reason, it's not being wasted.

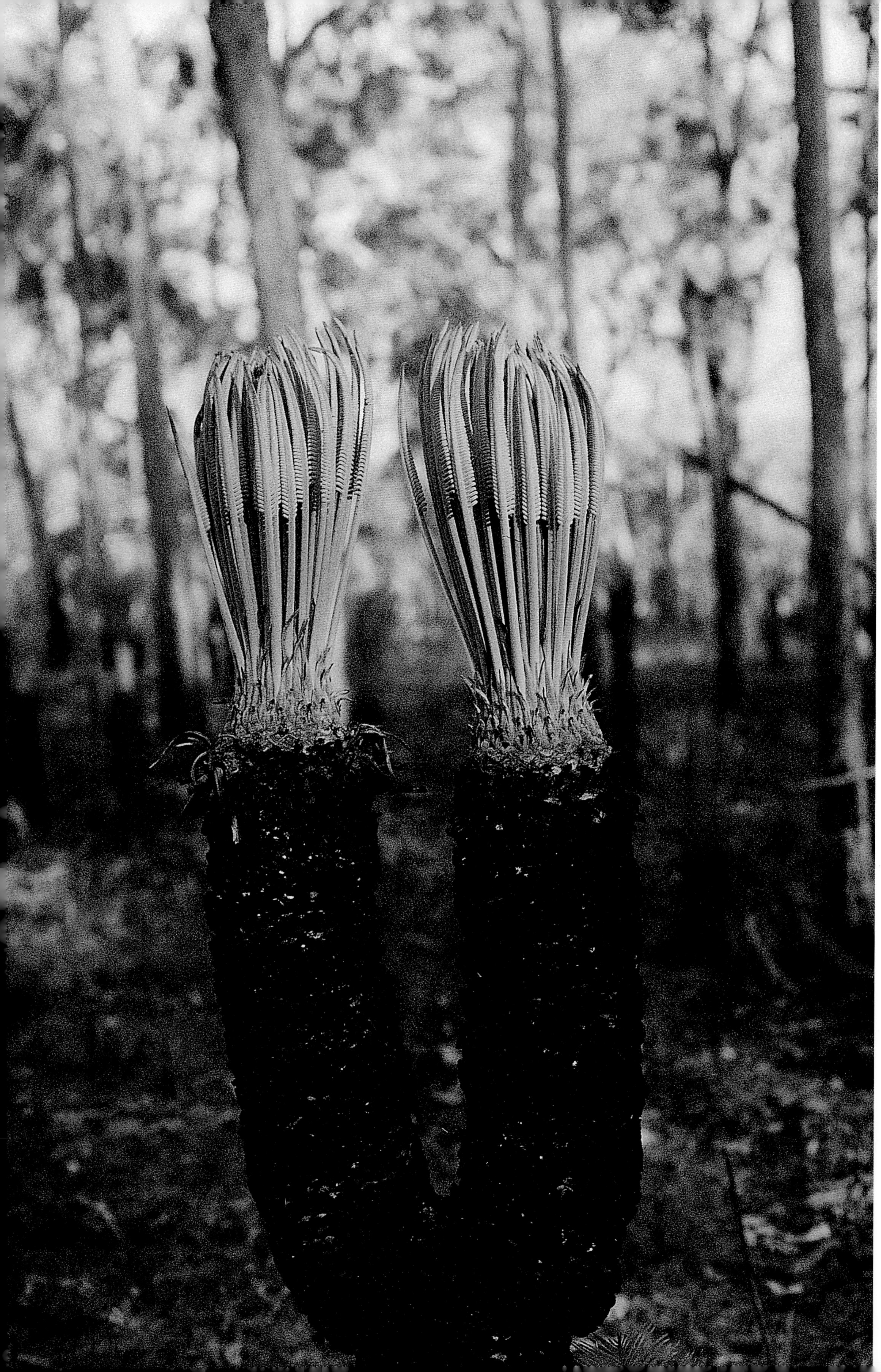

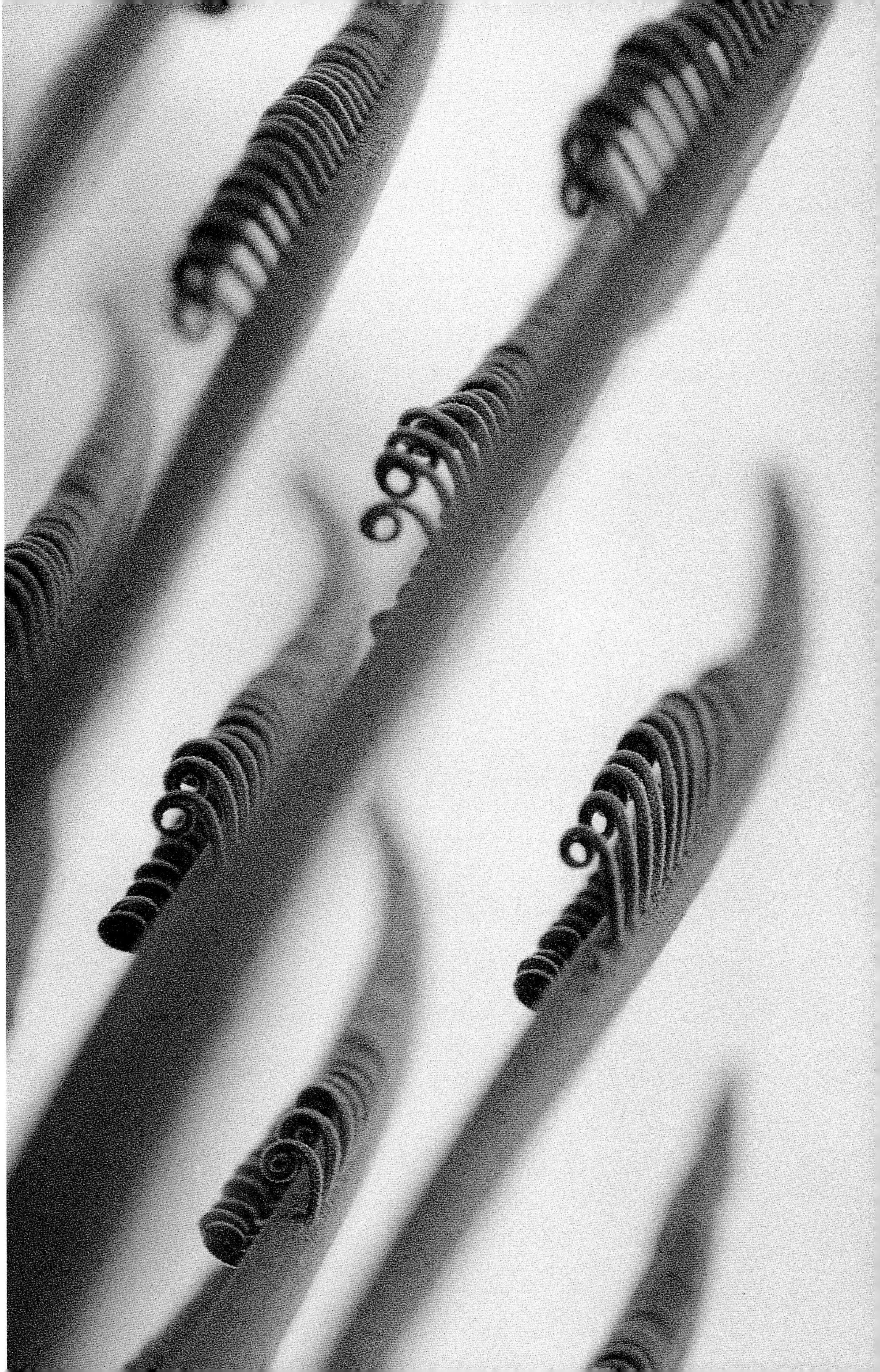

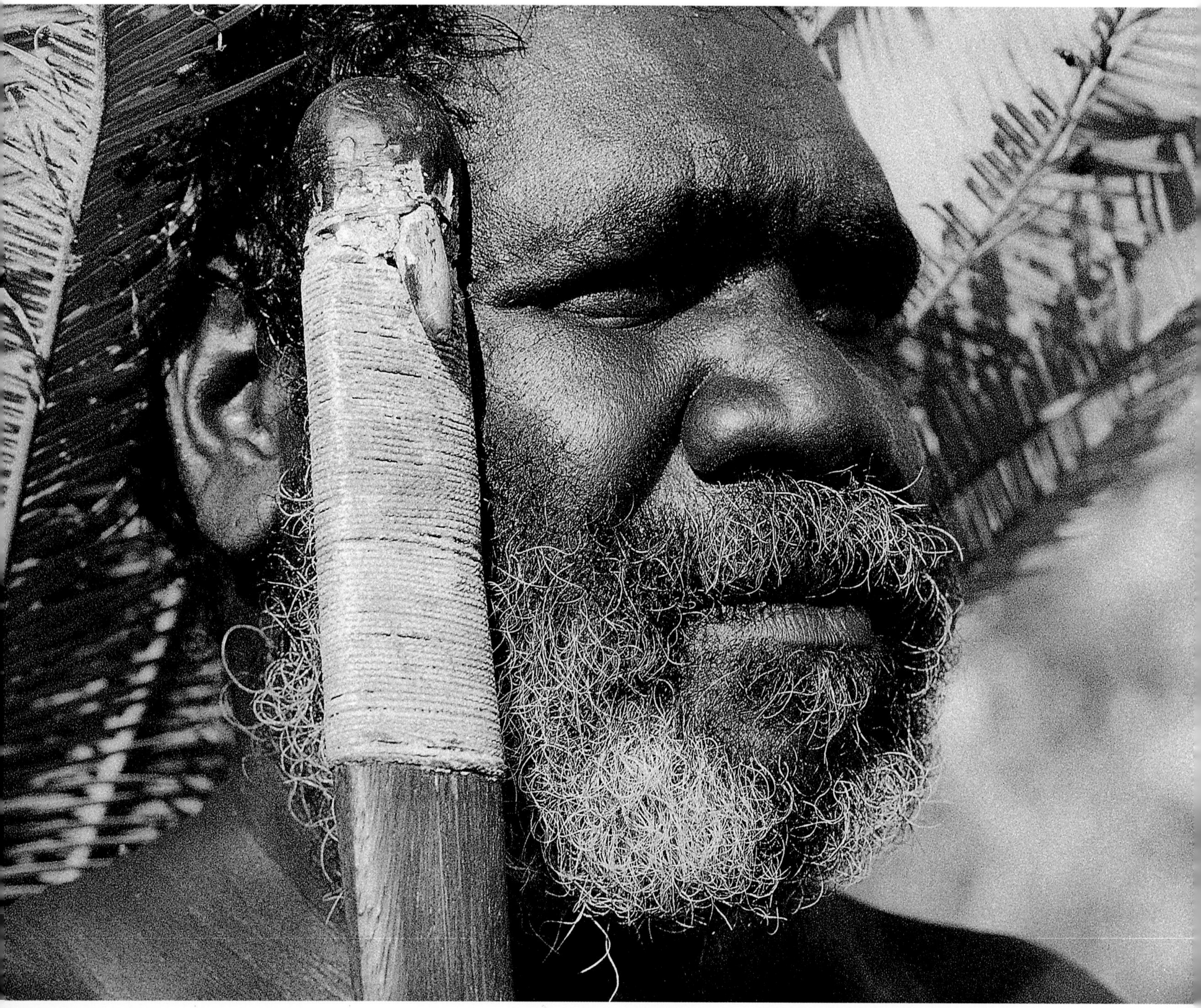

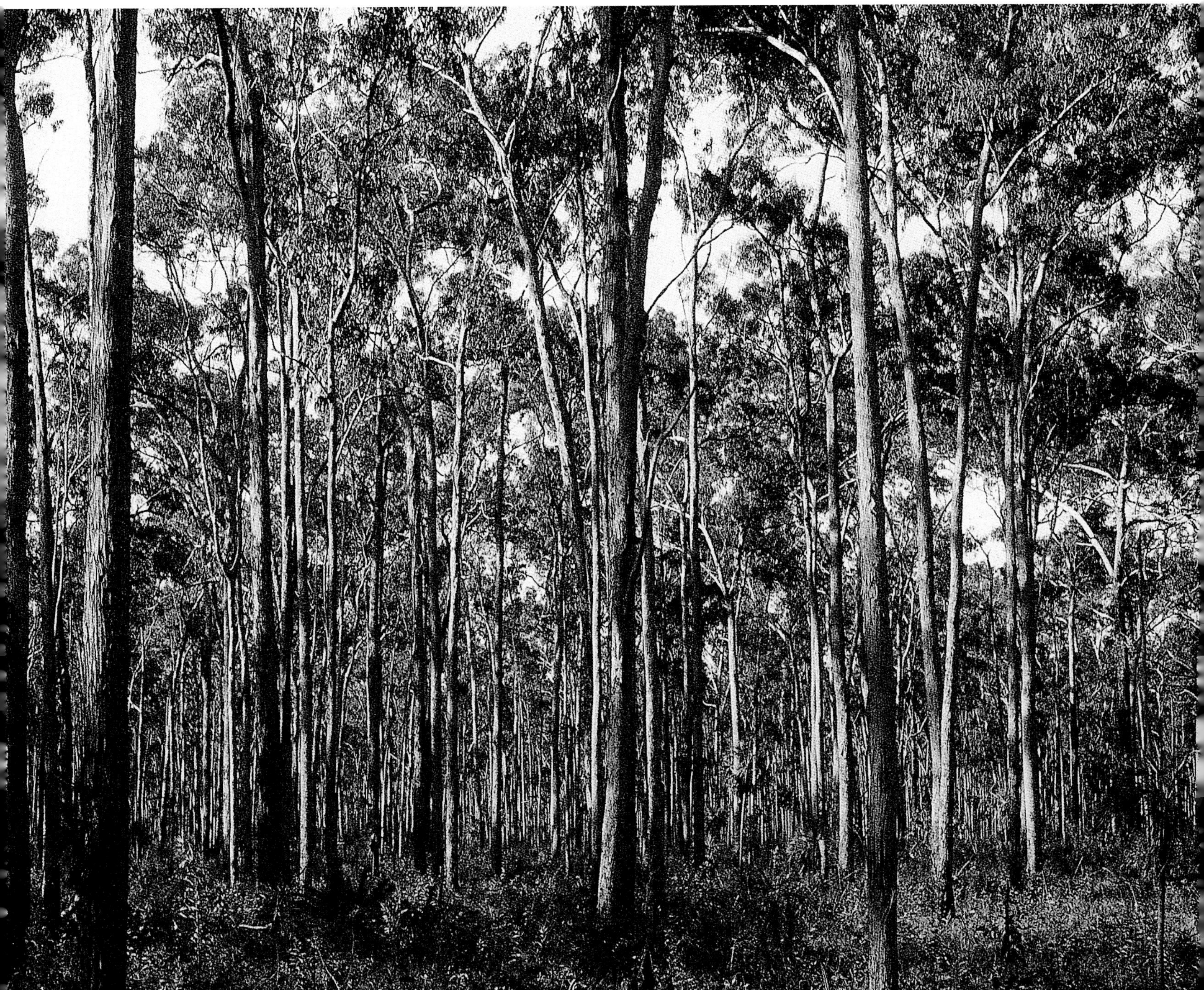

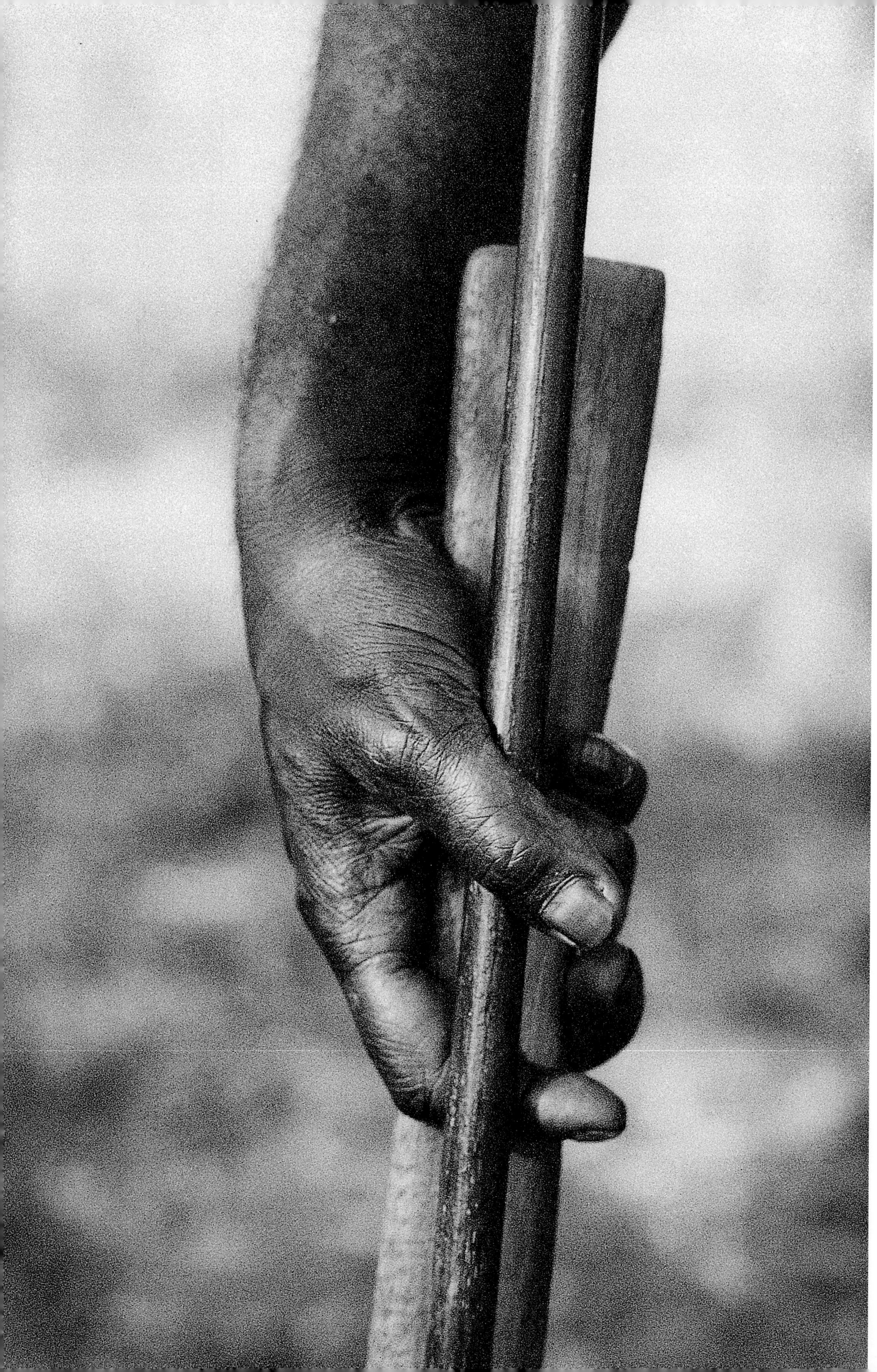

WARRIOR

Men get painted for battle, the other tribe will paint the same way. Mostly when they're going in to fight, it's a whole tribe, a big group going together. What if they were by themselves and a big group came? They'd have to run away, too dangerous. You have to know how to dodge a spear, break it or miss it.

To make yidaki, find a young stringybark tree, tap the tree to see it's hollow – that means termites inside – find a straight wood and clean it up. Make sure it's smooth for lips and play it straightaway. We use it at all ceremonies, but some songs we don't use yidaki for. Yidaki is mostly played in Arnhem Land.

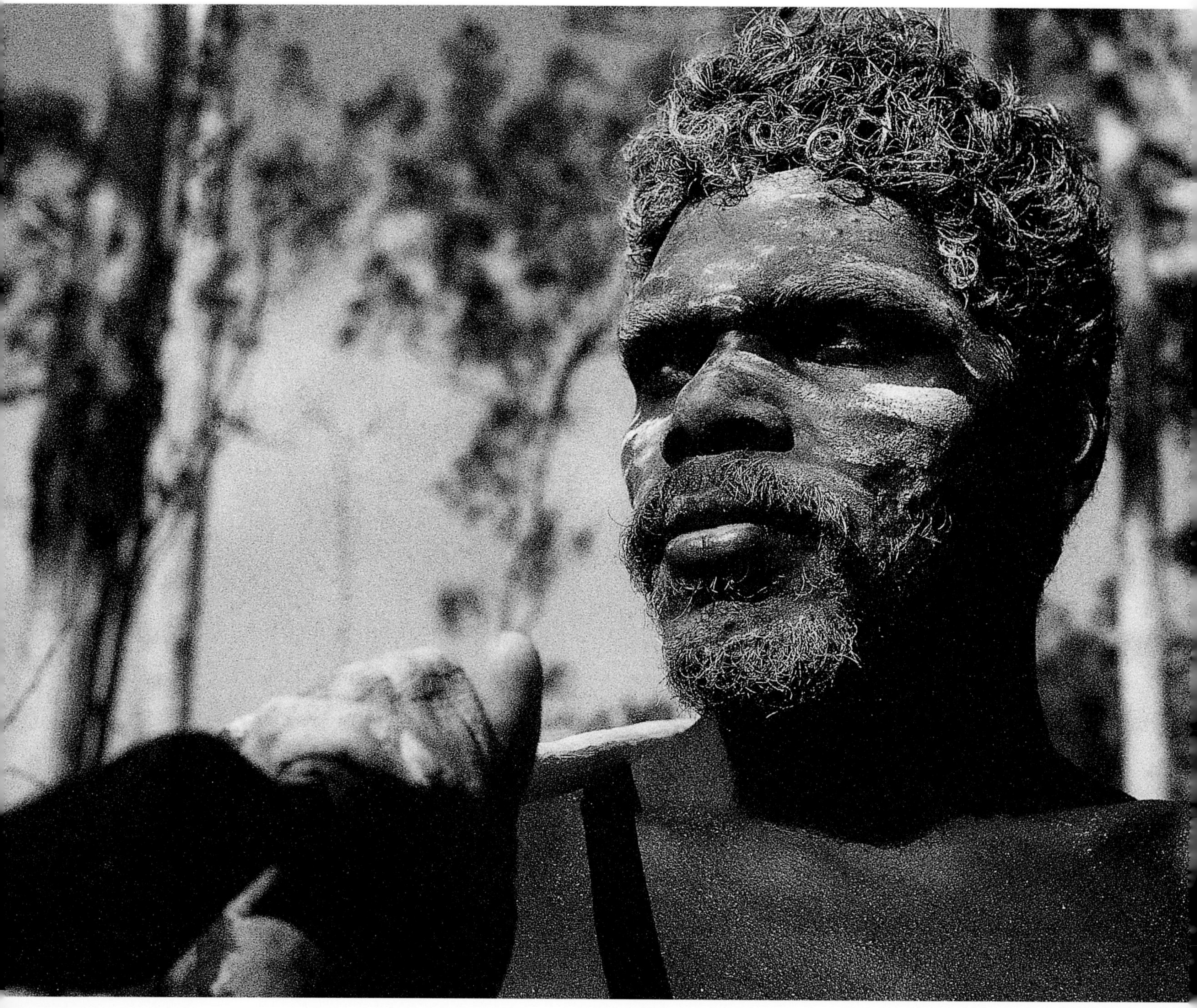

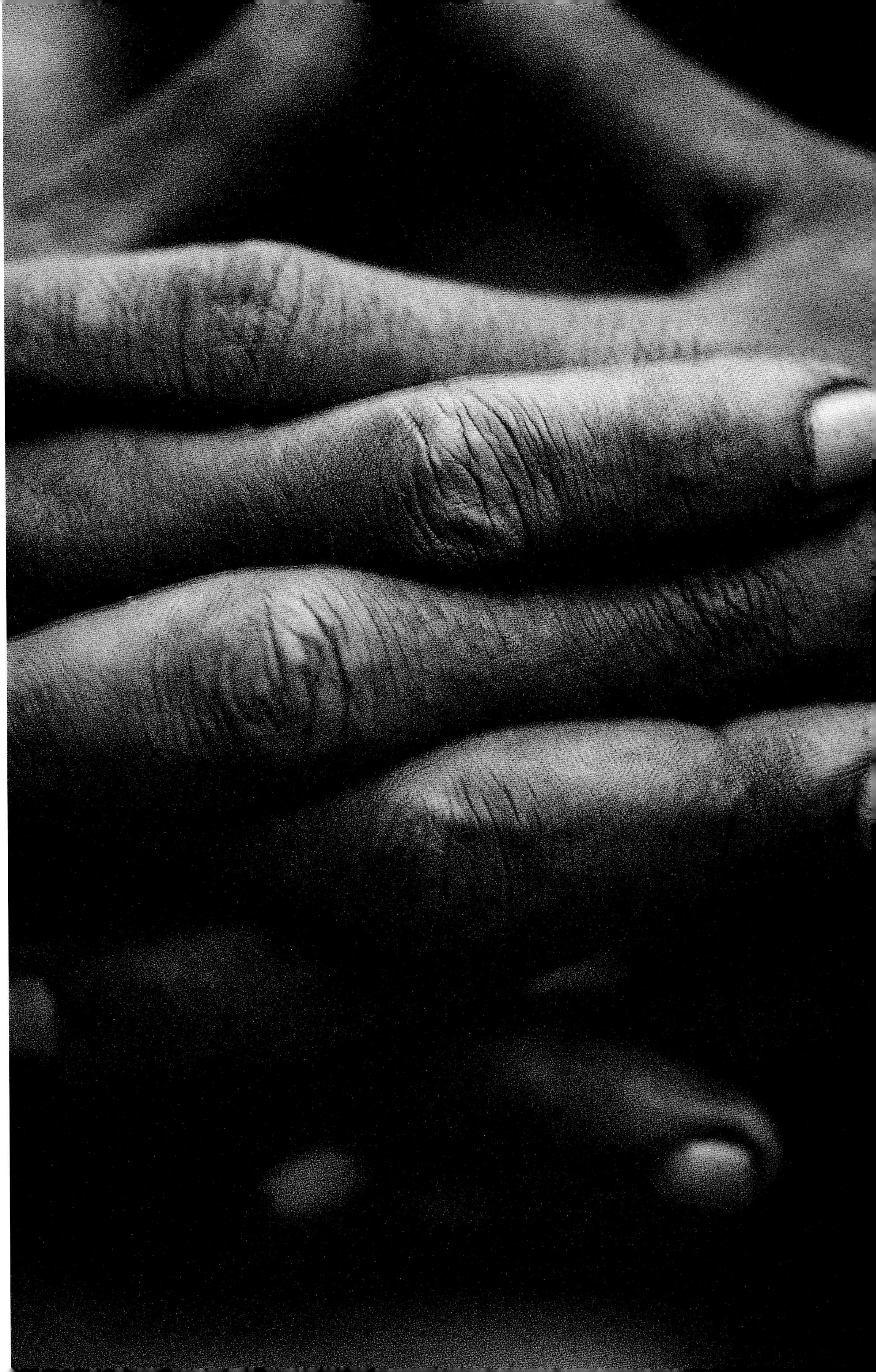

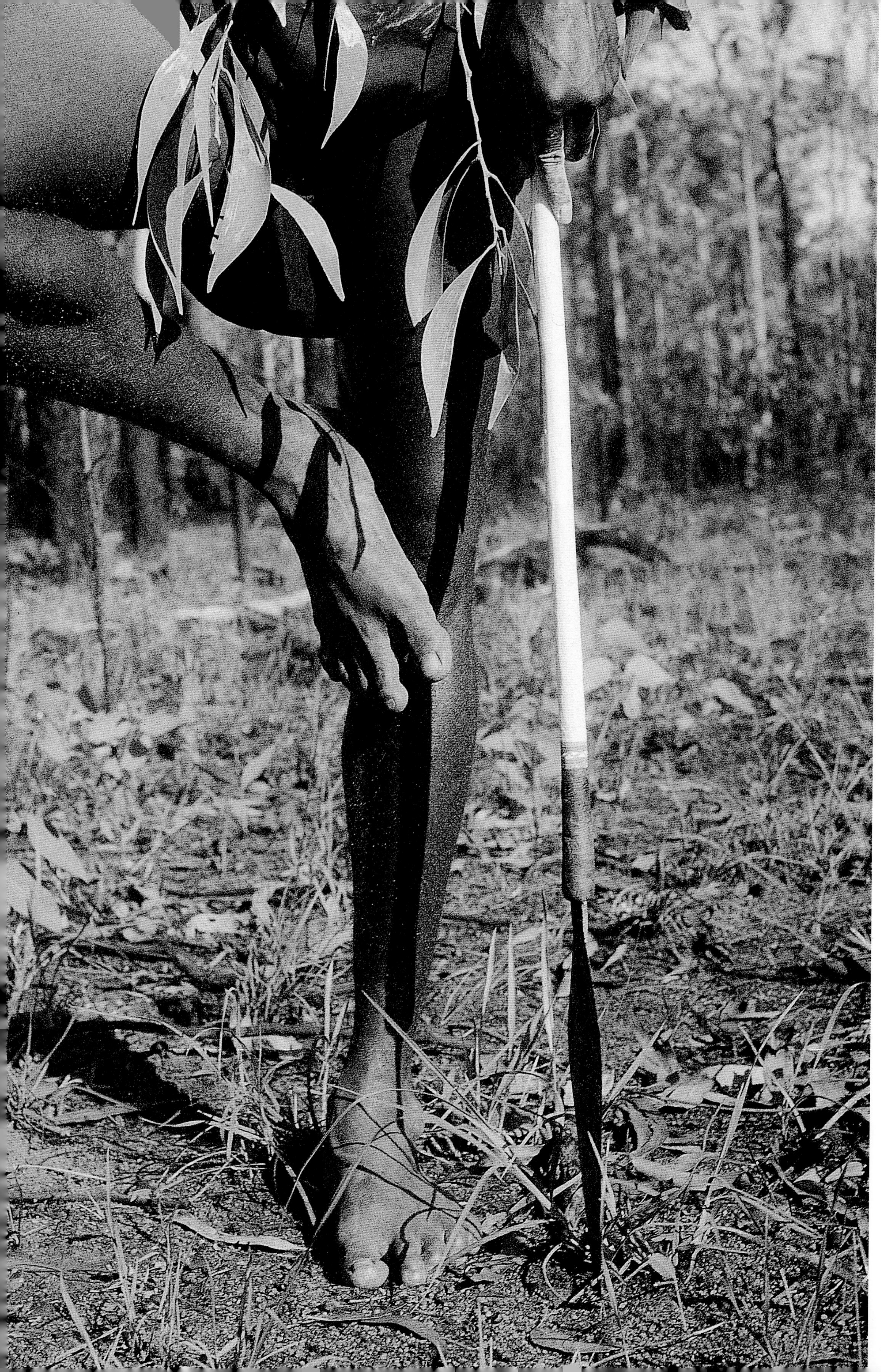

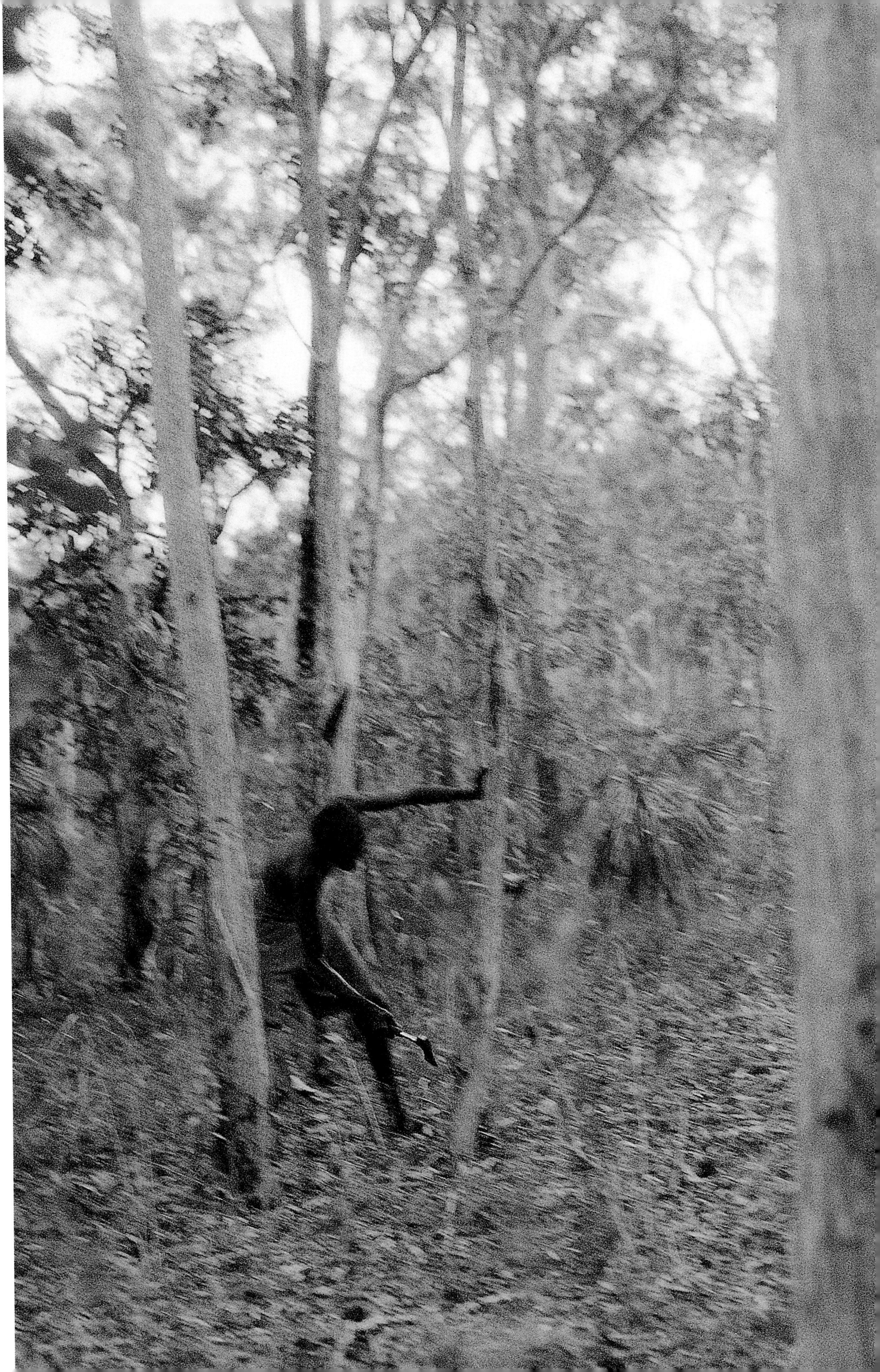

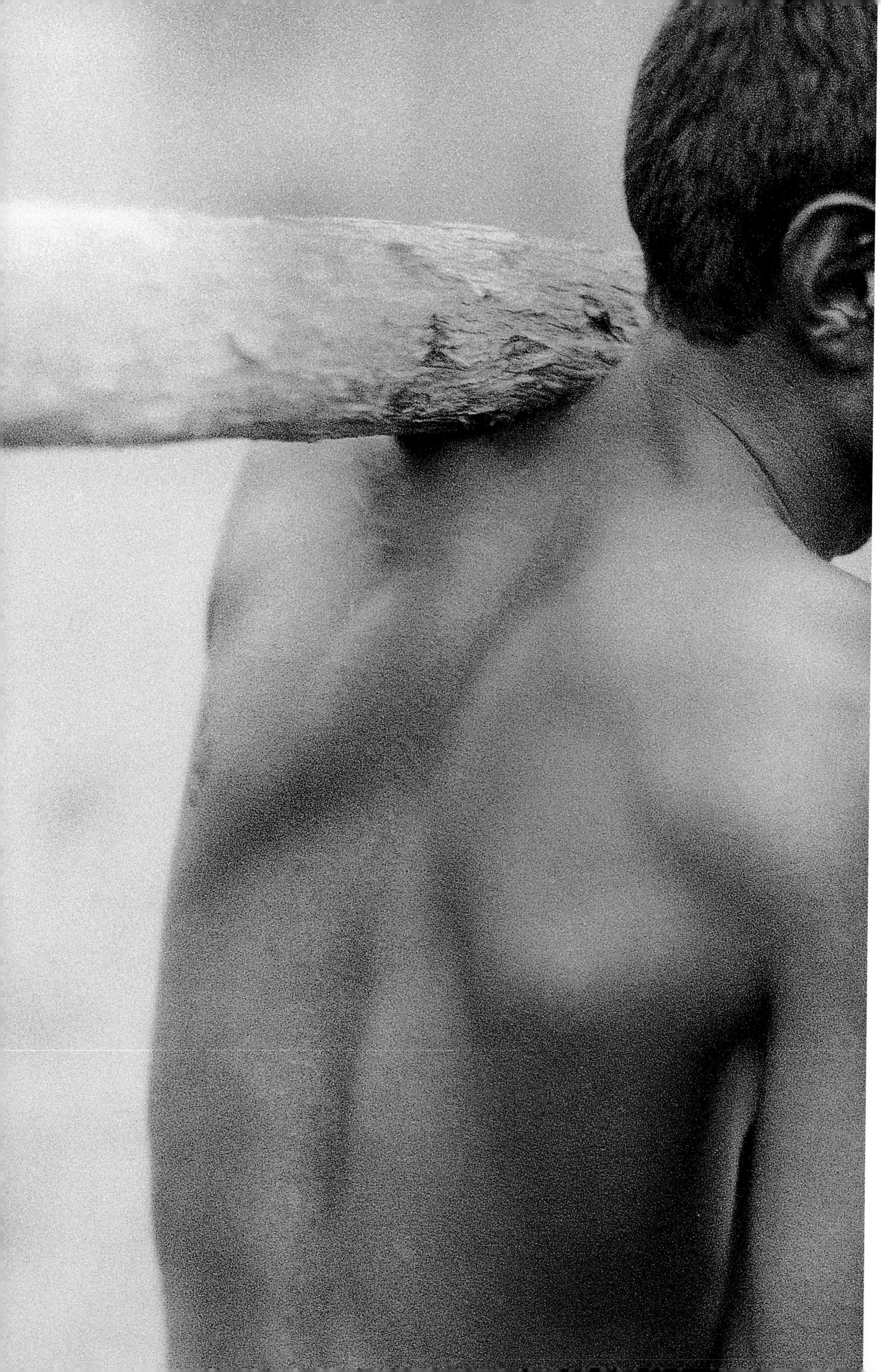

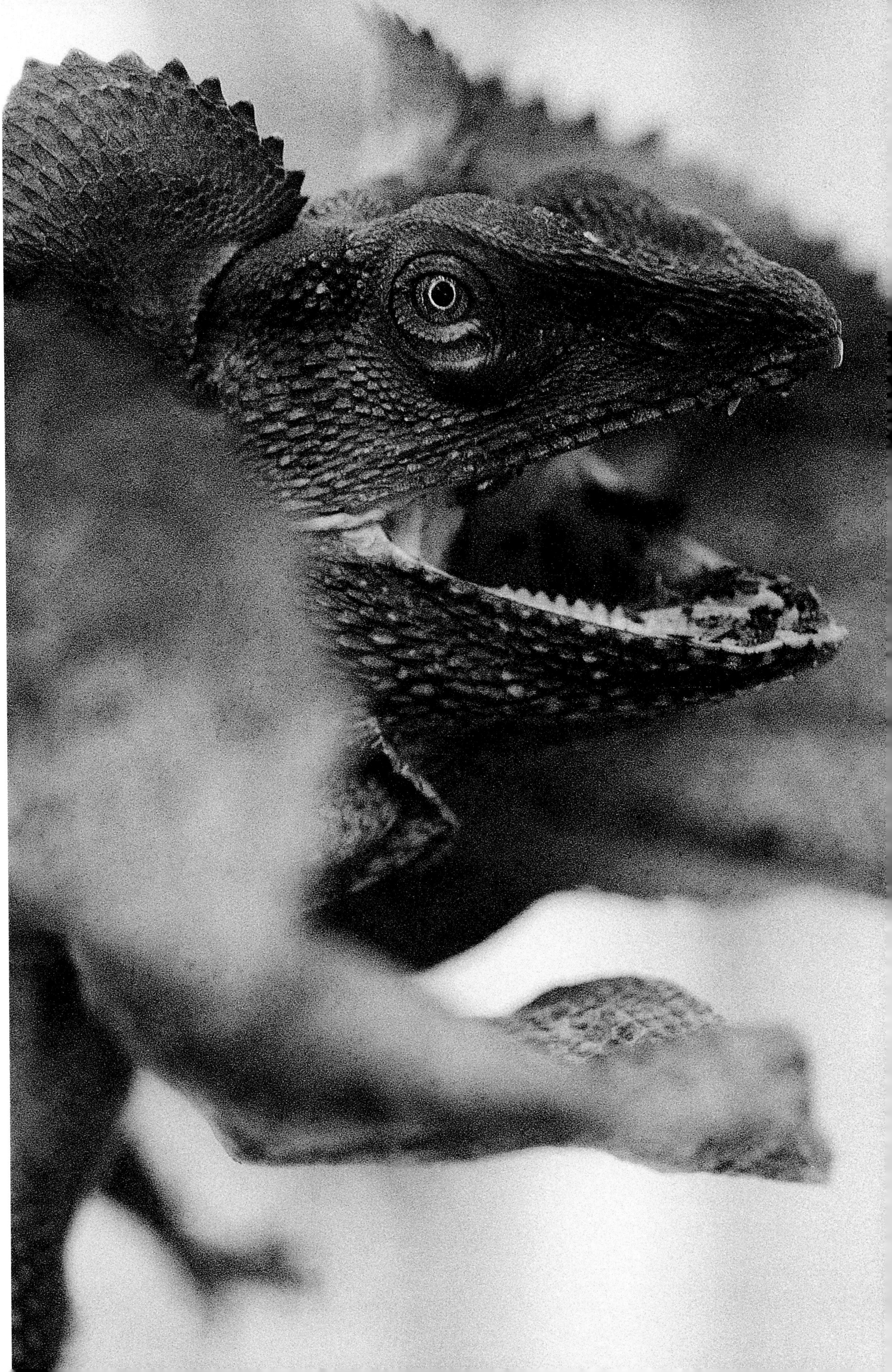

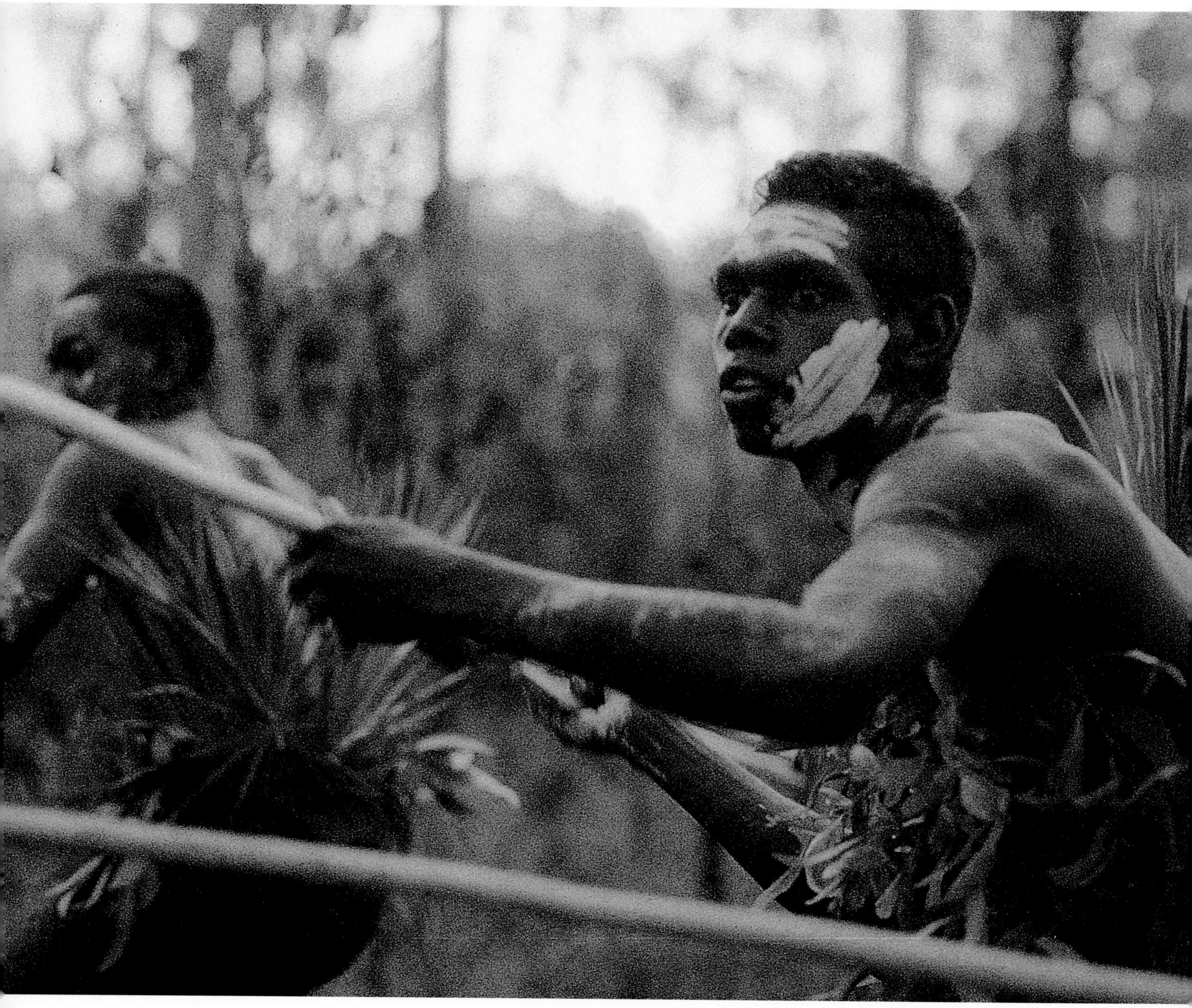

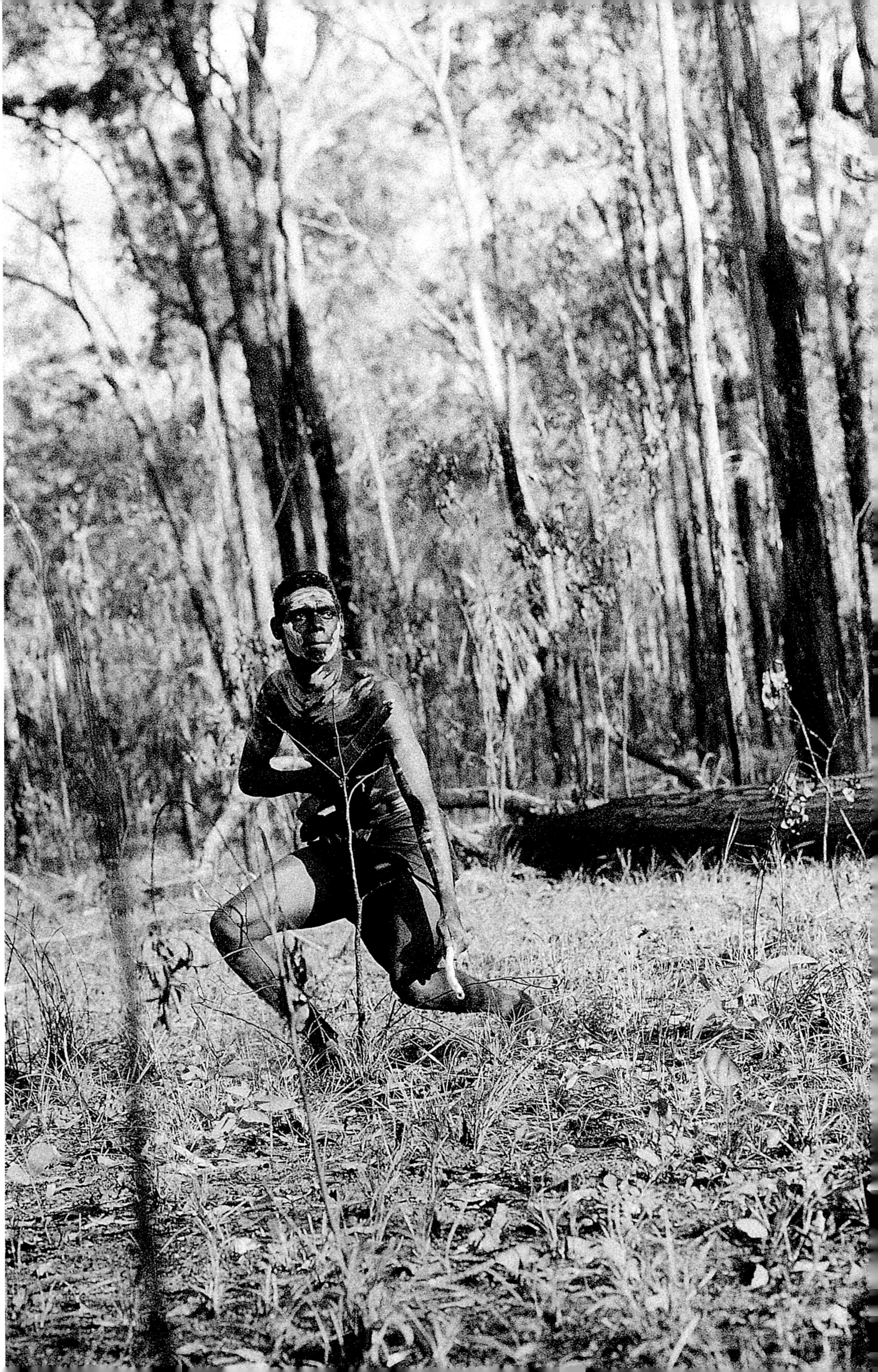

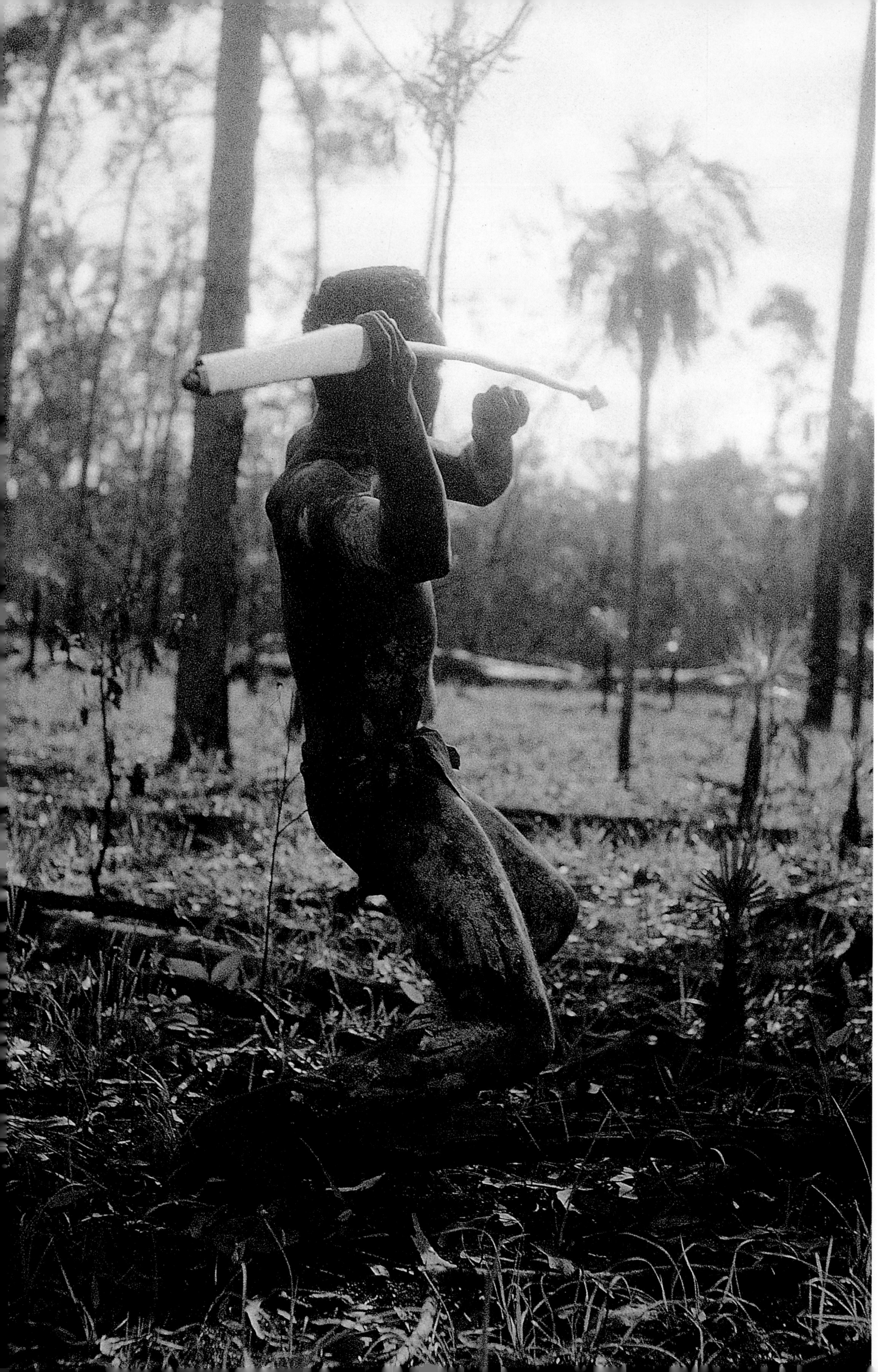

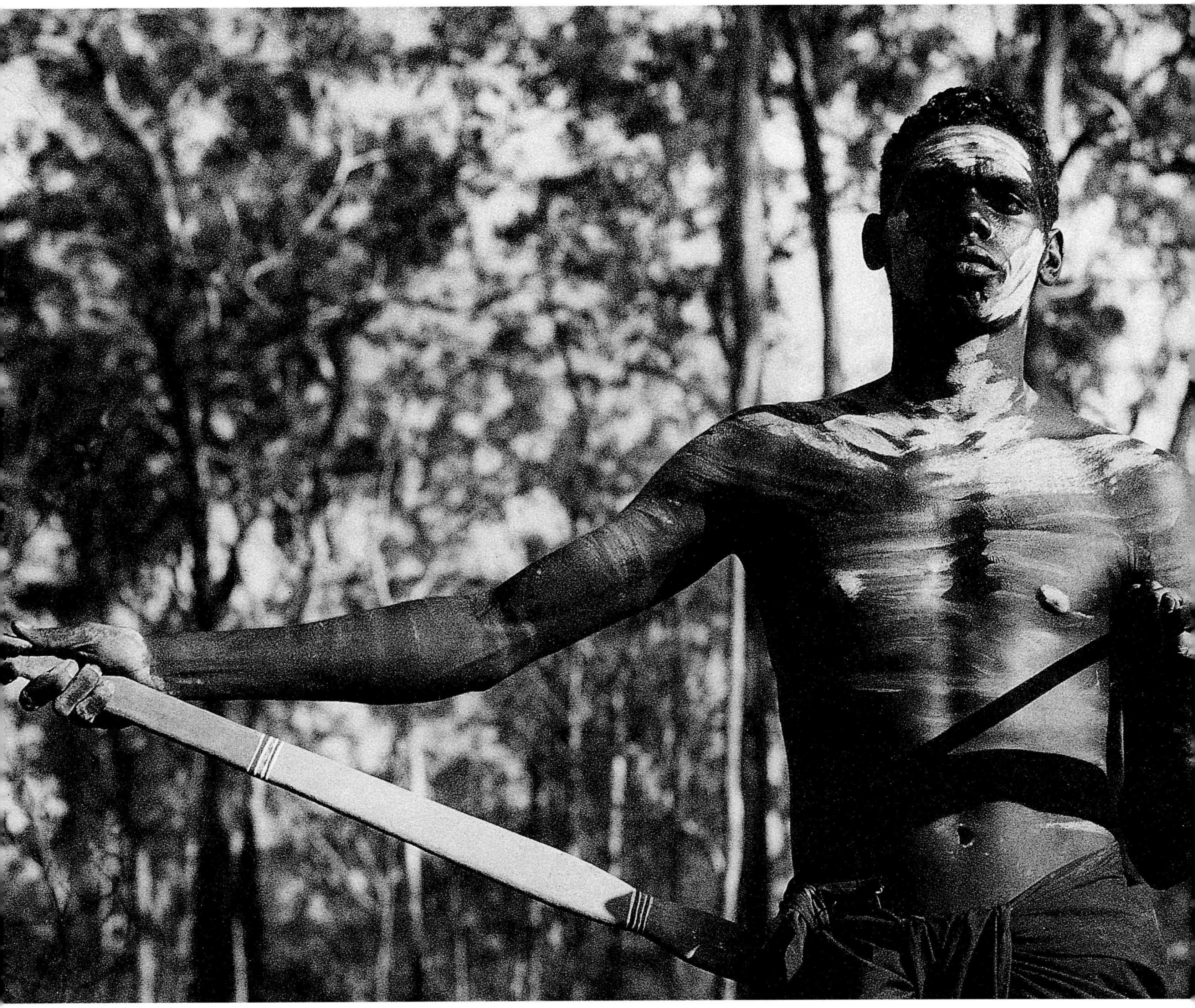

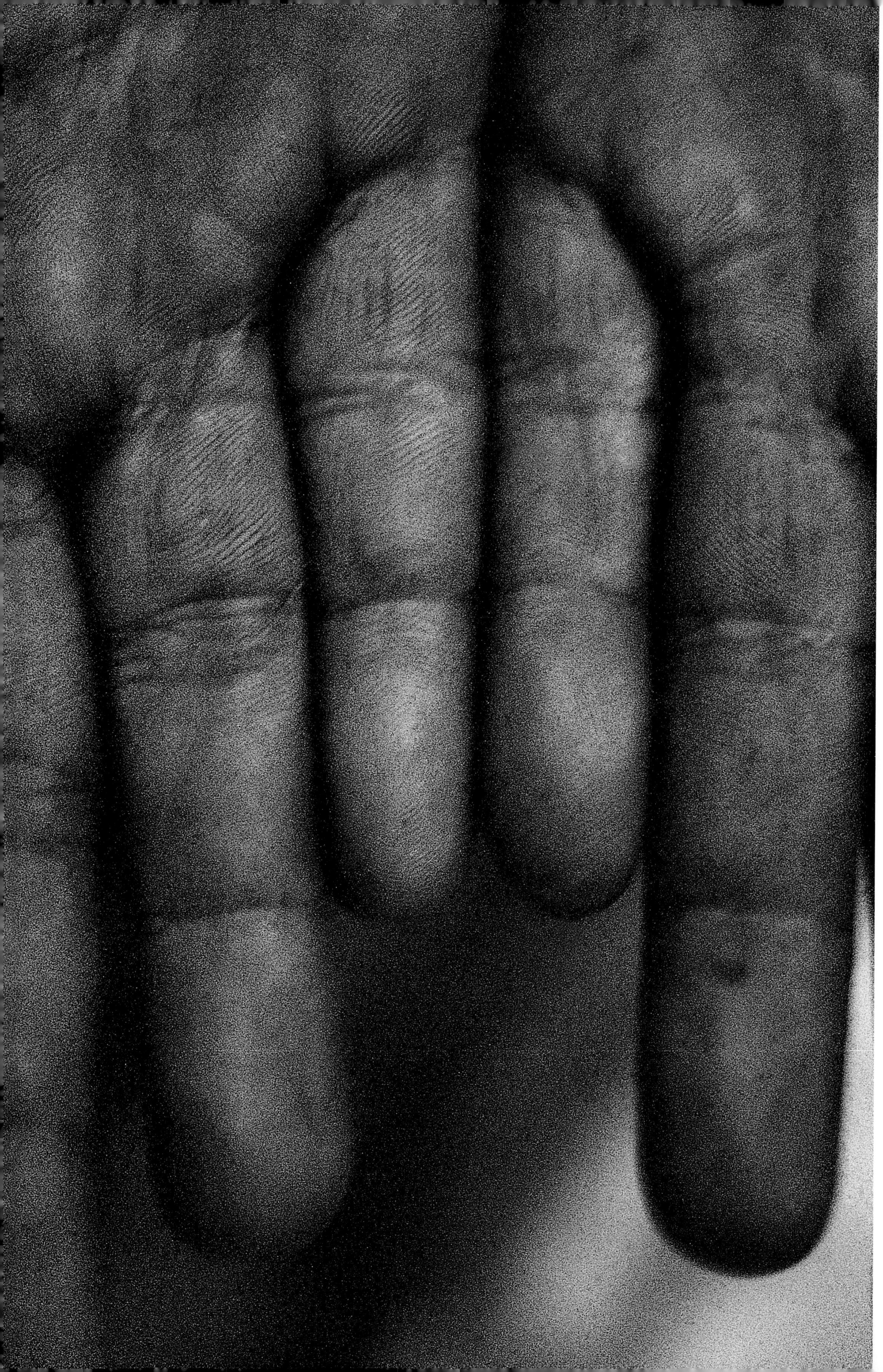

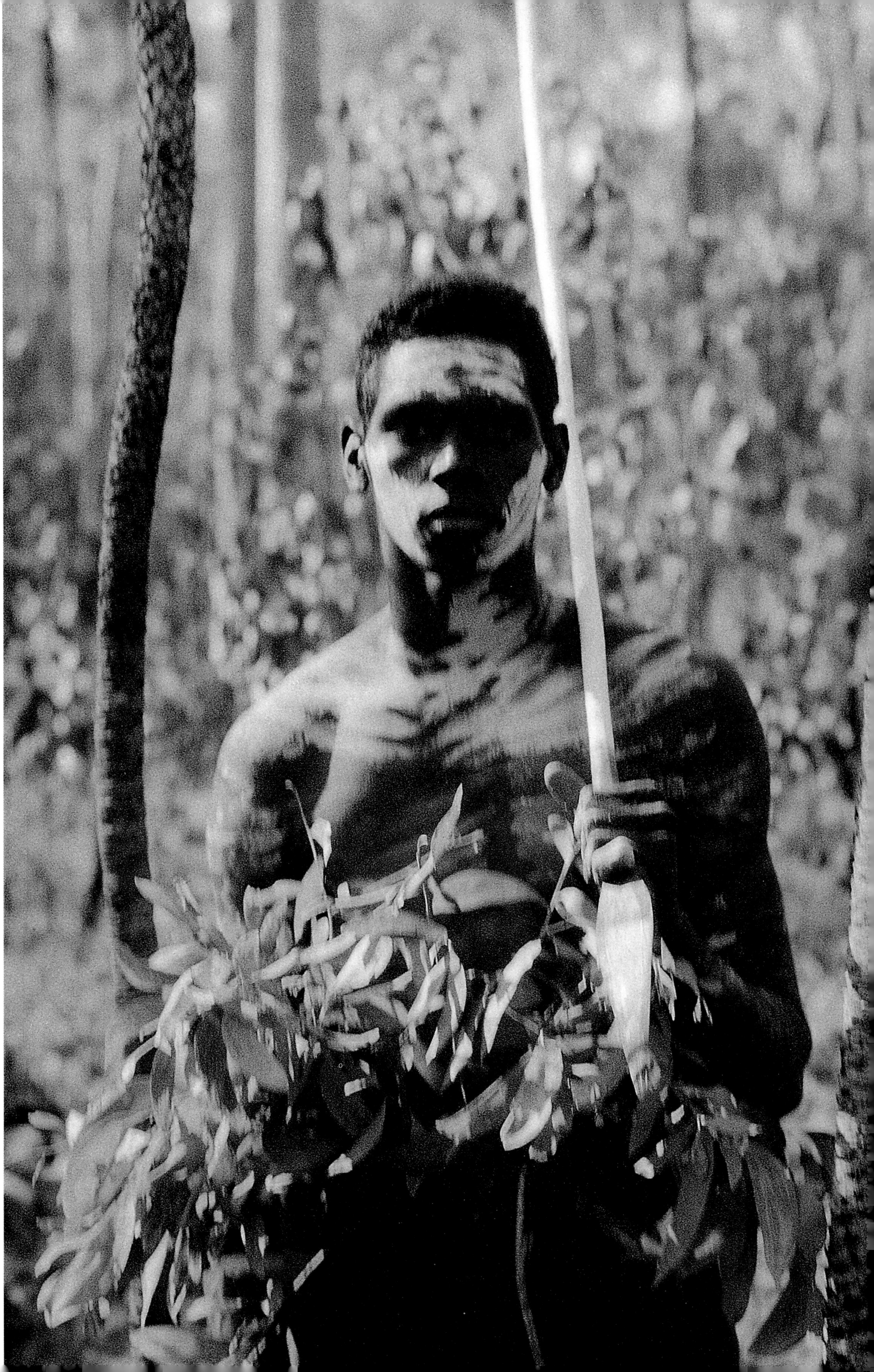

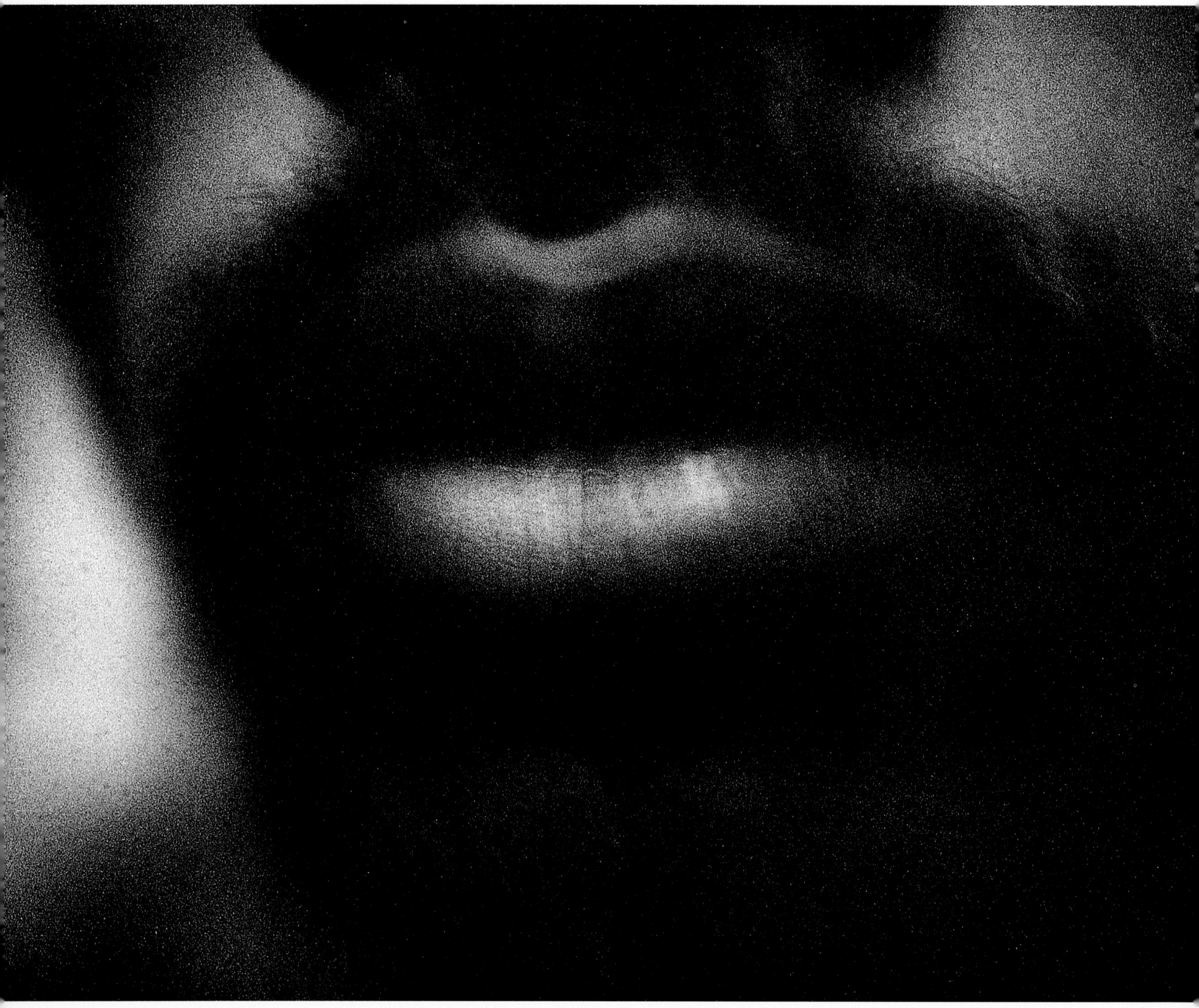

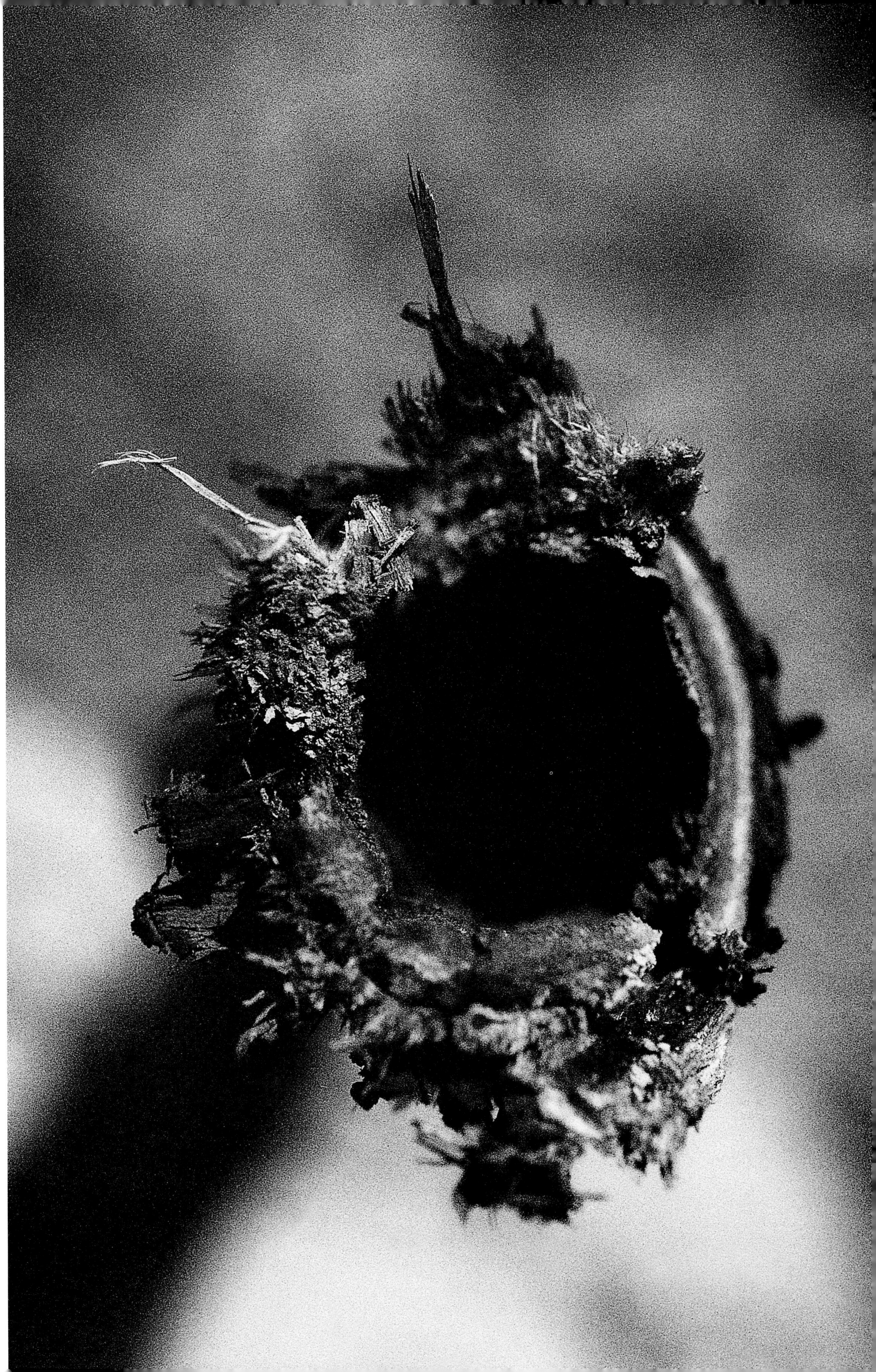

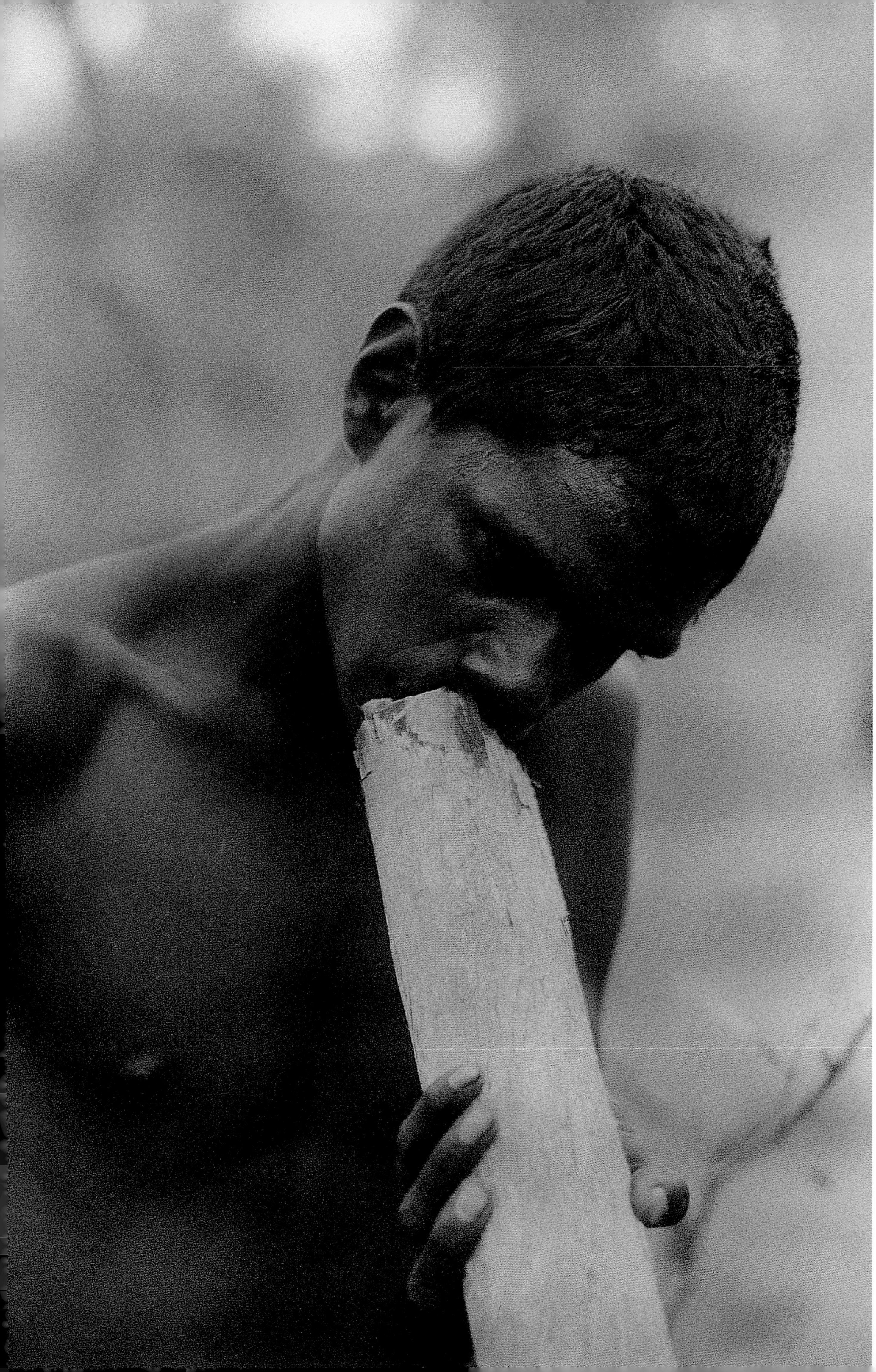

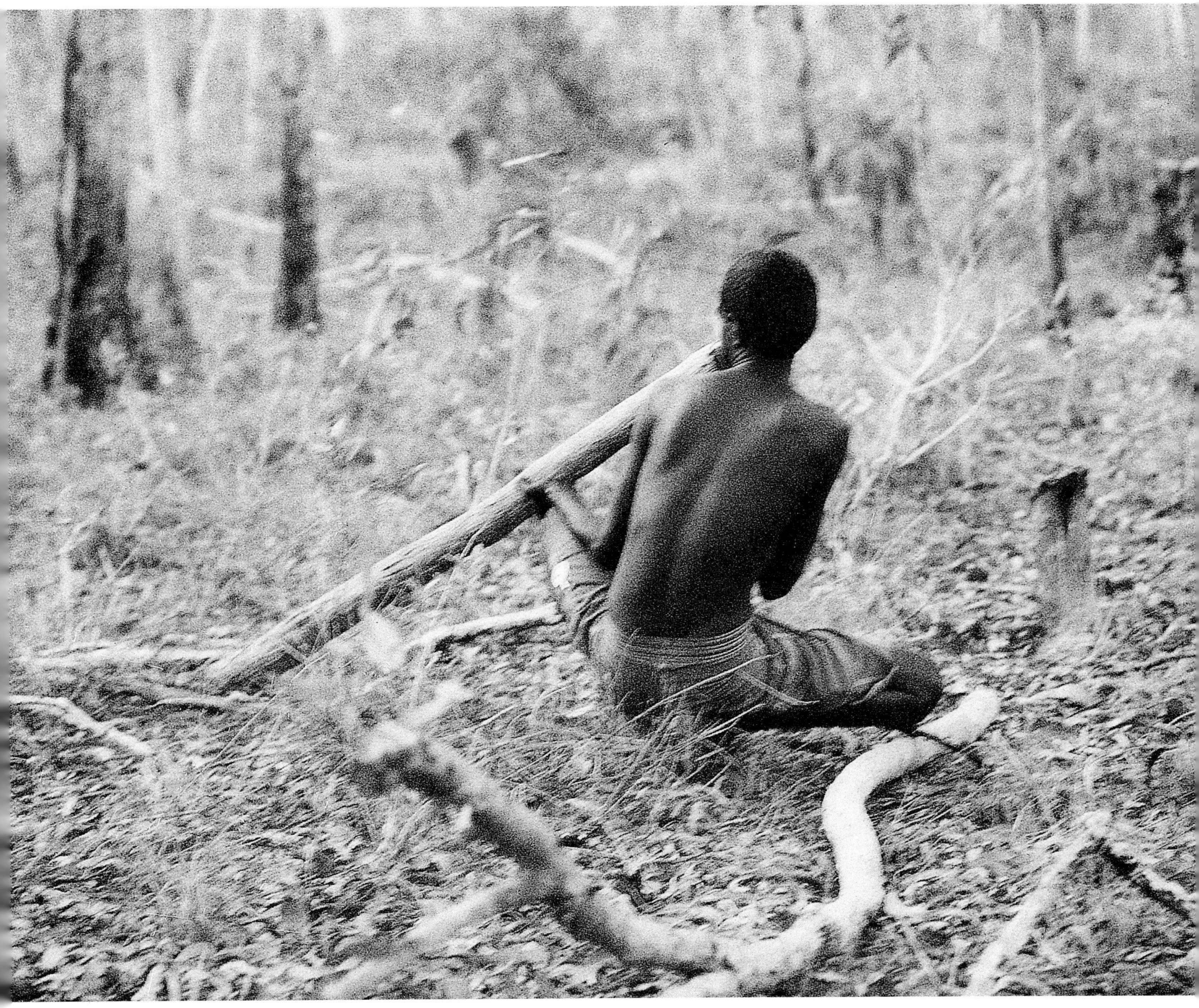

GLOSSARY

Balanda — a non-Indigenous person

Gäpirri — spotted stingray

Gumatj — the name of a clan group of the Yolngu

Yidaki — didgeridoo

Yirritja and Dhuwa the names of the two Yolngu moieties. Every person and perceptible entity is one or the other. Each person's moiety identity, Yirritja or Dhuwa, is inherited from their father. The universe is a harmonious whole composed of the two complementary halves.

LIST OF PHOTOGRAPHS

OUR CHILDREN

Ruby

Vision

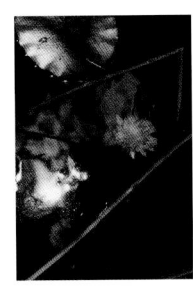

Gravity

Spirit of Possum

Yolngu Child

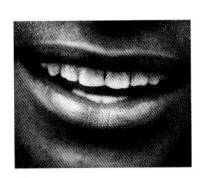

Lip

Brothers

Yirrkala

The Diver

New Beginning

Bliss

Young Turtle

GROWING UP

Baby Emus

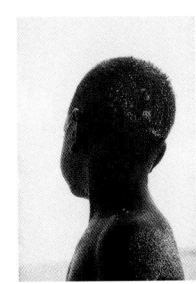

Skin

Buffalo Vision

Burning

Young Boy

Young Kangaroo

Microfeather

Shadow Mask

The Lizard

FAMILY STORIES

Father and Son  | Tradition 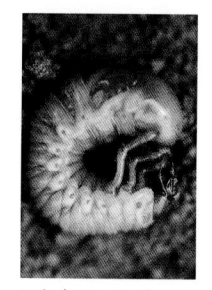 | Witchetty Grub  | Digging for Roots  | Emu Claw  | Drying Before Weaving

Roots for Dye  | Happiness  | Wisdom

CEREMONY

Manhood 1  | Manhood 2 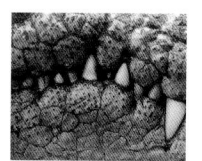 | Old Croc  | Cloud Pattern  | Young Crocs

TIMELESS WOMEN

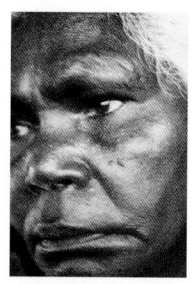

The Artist  | Gali Kali  | Oyster Meat  | Bush Apples  | Beauty 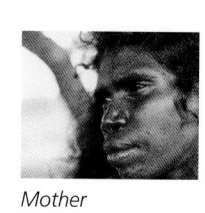 | Mother

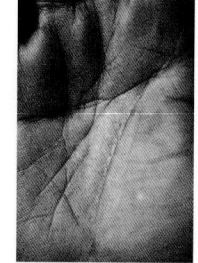

Palm 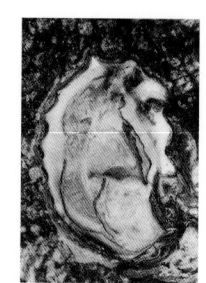 | Rock Oyster  | Mud Mussels 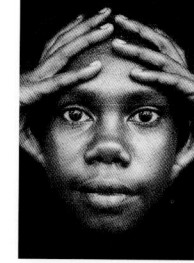 | Portrait  | Looking to the Sun

FLOWERS, STINGRAYS AND TURTLES

Skill

Urchin

Four Stingrays

Cutting Out the Barb

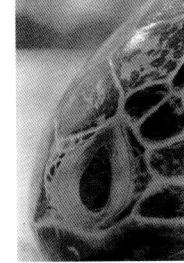

Old Turtle

Turtle Eggs

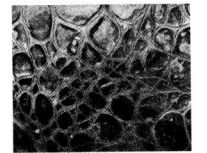

Turtle Skin

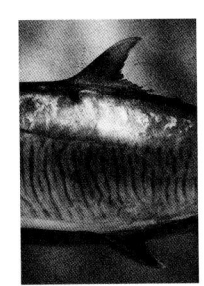

Mackerel Skin

Flower in Bloom

With Respect

Homeland

FLYING FOX

Flying Fox

In Flight

Escape

Hand of the Flying Fox

Mosquito Creek

WILD HONEY

Energy Food

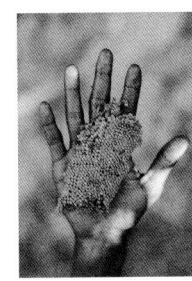

Wild Honey

Hunting Honey

Eating Fish

Nature's Way

Honey Tree

Snacking

Opening

A Friend

KANGAROO HUNTER

Food for All  *Carrying Roo*  *Man, Kangaroo, Spear*  *Cleaning Roo*  *Ribcage of Roo*

AFTER BUSHFIRE

Cycad After Bushfire  *New Shoots (Cycad)*  *Traditional Man*  *Stringybark Forest*  *Spear and Woomera in Hand*

WARRIOR

Battle 1 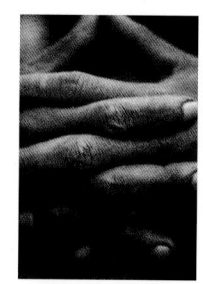 *Rest*  *Shovel-Nose Spear*  *Cutting Yidaki* 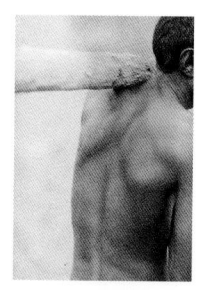 *Carrying Yidaki*  *Frill-Necked Lizard*

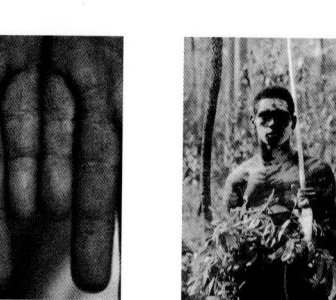

Moving In   *Battle 2*  *On Target* *Pride* *Two Hands* *Warrior*

Young Man 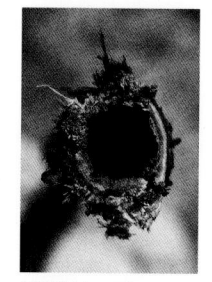 *Yidaki Just Cut*  *Testing Yidaki*  *A Good Yidaki*

The Yothu Yindi Foundation was incorporated as an Aboriginal Corporation in November 1990. It was established by Yolngu community leaders and persons of authority from five of the clan groups in the region. Broadly, its aims are to support and further the maintenance, development, teaching and enterprise potential of Yolngu cultural life.

For further information on the Yothu Yindi Foundation and its annual Garma Festival, visit www.yothuyindi.com and www.garma.telstra.com